SLOWPOKE

ONE NATION, OH MY GOD!

JEN SORENSEN

PUBLISHING

BROOKLYN, NEW YORK

SLOWPOKE

ONE NATION, OH MY GOD!

First edition
10 9 8 7 6 5 4 3 2 1
Printed in Canada

Ig Publishing
178 Clinton Avenue
Brooklyn, NY 11205

Visit the Slowpoke website at
www.slowpokecomics.com

LIBRARY OF CONGRESS CATALOGING-IN-PUBLICATION DATA:

Sorensen, Jen.
Slowpoke. One nation, oh my God! / Jen Sorensen.
p. cm.
ISBN-13: 978-0-9788431-6-8
ISBN-10: 0-9788431-6-9
1. United States--Politics and government--2001---Caricatures and cartoons.
2. United States--Social conditions--1980---Caricatures and cartoons.
3. Political culture--United States--Caricatures and cartoons.
4. Popular culture--United States--Caricatures and cartoons.
5. Editorial cartoons--United States.
6. American wit and humor, Pictorial.
I. Title.
II. Title: One nation, oh my God!
E902.S658 2008
741.5'973--dc22
2008004043

INTRODUCTION
Ruben Bolling, creator of "Tom the Dancing Bug"

You may know Jen Sorensen as a supremely talented humorist, a cartoonist who can take an inspired comedic premise, wrestle it to the ground, squeeze several top-notch gags out of it, and then force it to relinquish a payoff that is not only surprising and hilarious, but also often profound. Her *Slowpoke* comic strip is a paradigm of the form of alternative political cartooning.

But as another practicing cartoonist, I simply know her as a colleague and fellow practitioner of the Art. It's easy to imagine us as gods and goddesses sitting high upon a mountain, observing the human condition, and dropping sweet humor-tinged nectar drops of insight upon those who dwell below. But in fact, we're just regular workaday people who happen to have gifts so special that it is easy for us to imagine things like that.

Perhaps a true story will illustrate my point. I like to get together with cartoonists as often as once every five years or so, to talk shop, commiserate on the skyrocketing cost of rapidograph ink, trade cartooning gossip, and discuss how to draw George Bush's ears. When the witticisms and profundities are being batted around by these giants of humor, I often wish I were a fly on the wall. Because frankly it can get pretty boring, and it's cool to imagine walking on walls!

During one of these gatherings, a conference of editorial cartoonists, I was walking through the hotel lobby when I saw Jen sitting in a chair clutching a notebook open to a page densely filled with sketches and jottings. As I took a seat across from her, she told me that she was on deadline, and had to finish writing a comic strip, in part about the Beatles.

I laughed heartily. Who knows where our respective muses will take us in any given week? Jen seemed puzzled by my hearty laughter, and eager to resume her work, so I dialed down to a knowing chuckle, and began to take my leave.

Now, as something of an elder statesman in the field of producing weekly multi-panel cartoons of socio-political satire that appear mostly in alternative weekly newsprint publications and that feature intermittently used recurring characters, I felt I should offer some guidance to my struggling colleague. Luckily, I've got the finely honed razor-sharp instincts for humor of a very humorous jungle cat.

So, as I left, I leaned in and said, "Ringo is the funniest Beatle. Try to use Ringo." If only one of our biographers were present to witness this moment. Jen's smile was as mysterious and inscrutable as the smile Leonardo Da Vinci must have had when he painted Mona Lisa's smile. Was it a smile of recognition of the essential secrets all humorists share? Was it a smile acknowledging the cosmic truth and power of humor? Or was it a polite smile that attempted to end this exchange so that she could get back to finish her comic? I don't think I'll ever know.

She pleasantly responded, "I've already got a Ringo joke in there." Ah, can the master teach a master? Of course not.

I walked outside the hotel, only to be greeted by several autograph seekers who, in their trepidation to approach me, covered their embarrassment by shouting past me to the members of the Chicago Cubs baseball team who happened to be staying at the same hotel. I laughed heartily, drawing more puzzled looks.

So, as you read and enjoy this book, stand not in awe of Jen Sorensen's powers. Yes, she'll make you laugh, and make you think, and you'll be thoroughly entertained. But the Ringo joke was pretty much written by me.

Ruben Bolling
Bowman, North Dakota

FOREWORD

It's a common refrain among political cartoonists that today's killer strip is tomorrow's fishwrap, its subject matter old news before the ink fully dries. I disagree. To wrap fish, I recommend a heavy freezer paper devoid of newsprint, sealed with tape and carefully dated. But even if you only have the back section of your local alternative newsweekly, the part where our cartoons normally appear alongside reams of enormous sex-ad hooters—even then, I would urge you to spare Slowpoke from the tilapia slime. After all, someone in your family might want the 900 number just beneath it.

I, for one, think good political cartoons retain their value for decades. You can learn a lot from those old "Doonesbury" books. I might add that we cartoonists who lambasted the Bush administration from the beginning have been proven more accurate than most of the highly-paid gasbags you see on television. Historians and television producers, please take note.

It's true, certain references will inevitably be lost on readers over time. That's why I've decided to add a new piece of Cartoon Book Technology to this collection: written commentary for every strip. You'll find all sorts of contextual background, fun facts, and exclusive peeks into the high-rolling lifestyle of a self-syndicated altweekly cartoonist. The strips themselves are arranged largely in chronological order, beginning with the period just before the 2004 elections. As we enter a new election cycle, these cartoons remain distressingly relevant.

Many cartoons in this book are not overtly political. One can only write so many strips about torture before one needs to lighten up with a riff on Gucci flipflops. Lots of people seem to think we cartoonists will be struggling for material when Bush leaves office, but I will personally be relieved to get off this spiraling Swift Boat to hell. Even if the next administration is as corrupt as ever, at least it will be one that disgusts and appalls in new ways, opening up a wealth of fresh comedic possibilities.

For those new to Slowpoke, that pointy-headed character you see in so many cartoons is Mr. Perkins. In his natural state, he is a prim, mildly anxious gentleman in an orange flannel suit, married to one Mrs. Perkins, who makes her debut in this collection. Mr. Perkins is under my employ as a kind of cartoon actor; I place him in a variety of roles, many of them unsavory (such as our current potentate), but some quite sane (Professor Perkins). Rest assured, he is amply compensated for his thespian endeavors.

It may interest you to know some of the lesser titles that were rejected for this book: *Welcome to the Bungle; The Lighter Side of Impending Doom;* and *Floozies, Doozies, and Salad Uzis.* In the end, I think my publisher and I made the right decision. I'm already looking forward to the potential Spanish-language translation: *Un Nación, ¡Dios Mío!*

Jen Sorensen
Charlottesville, Virginia
February, 2008

ACKNOWLEDGMENTS

The following people deserve a round of Victory Storm King Imperial Stouts: Ruben Bolling for his thoughtful introduction and for actually appreciating my holiday-themed reminders regarding its due date; Dan Perkins, Alison Bechdel, and Jim Hightower for their kind blurbage; Robert Lasner and Elizabeth Clementson of Ig Publishing for being open to doing a cartoon book and trusting me to put it together; and Sohrab Habibion for his layout and design assistance.

I would like to bestow a Fuller's 1845 Celebration Ale upon *C-VILLE Weekly* editor Cathy Harding for her sisterly support, letting me use her living room to get files for this book off my computer when I had a power outage, and not minding whatever destruction I did to her screen door last summer.

A bulbous flask of Kwak shall be served to Warren Bernard and his cats for their hospitality and support of political cartooning; and to the Cartoonists With Attitude for their camaraderie.

A tall Paulaner Hefeweizen with lemon wedge goes to editorial cartoonists Joel Pett, Matt Wuerker, Bill Day, and Clay Bennett for going out of their way to help.

A fragrant Belgian Trippel with a thunderous bouquet and notes of banana and cloves goes to Tom Hart and Tim Kreider for good times on the "Laugh While You Can" tour.

A shot of Green Spot to Adam for his mad programming skillz and horticultural advice.

A Lancaster Hop Hog to readers for their often-entertaining and informative emails.

A silky yet playful pinot noir to Mom, Dad, Pam, and Rick, for their love, encouragement, and patience with my sometimes-inconvenient deadlines.

And of course, Scott (a.k.a. "Mr. Slowpoke") gets a mammoth keg of Rodenbach Grand Cru for his help and for being an all-around excellent guy.

This book is dedicated to Scott and Carney.

My, how times change. Does anyone else remember when the concept of "freedom" was a lot more *Easy Rider* and a lot less *Terminator*? Not that I'm endorsing the "magic bus" version, as depicted in the first panel—but freedom used to feel a lot more laid-back, man.

I'm also tired of being called a "radical," a word that even many otherwise-astute progressives apply to themselves. Since when is it radical to not want mercury in my tuna salad? Or to have an aversion to killing tens of thousands of innocent civilians unnecessarily? I'm the normal person here. The people running the country are the off-the-meter nutballs.

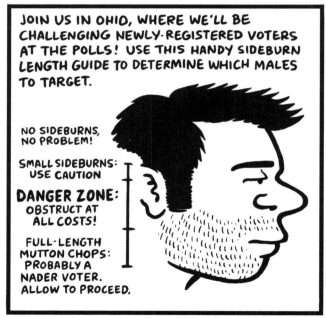

In the weeks leading up to Election Day, a spate of reports about possible shenanigans had me very worried. A Republican politician in Michigan had warned that his party would have a tough time if it did not "suppress the Detroit vote." Ohio Secretary of State and Bush-Cheney campaign co-chair Ken Blackwell had bizarrely rejected new voter registration cards not printed on 80-pound paper. The Ohio Republicans were also sending armies of challengers to predominantly-black precincts with the likely effect of slowing down already-long lines. Blackwell was later condemned for his violations of voter rights in a report issued by Rep. John Conyers of the House Judiciary Committee.

This cartoon came out of the controversy surrounding Dan Rather's report on Bush's spotty National Guard record. While the overall gist of the report was accurate, Rather mistakenly presented documents that many believe were forgeries. The resulting furor from Bush supporters ended Rather's career at CBS. Meanwhile, these same self-appointed stewards of journalistic integrity had little to say about the daily falsehoods spouted on Fox News, the Swift Boat Vets, or pundits such as Armstrong Williams who took payola from the Bush Administration. The 2004 presidential race and its appalling media coverage represented the absolute triumph of unreality in American politics.

more FRAMING FUNNIES

SOMEHOW, EATING HEALTHY HAS BEEN LABELLED "POLITICALLY CORRECT."

"BURGER KING IS GOING 180 DEGREES AWAY FROM POLITICALLY CORRECT FOOD."

A FAST FOOD INDUSTRY CONSULTANT ON B.K.'S "ENORMOUS OMELET SANDWICH" (ACTUAL QUOTE)

IT'S A CURIOUS LOGIC: IF IT'S GOOD FOR YOU, IT'S "PC."

THESE POLITICALLY CORRECT **BREATHING NAZIS!** I DON'T NEED THEIR DAMNED AIR.

I'LL SHOW **THEM!**

...URK! MAYBE NOT.

THE WAY THINGS ARE GOING, GROCERY STORES WILL SOON LOOK LIKE THIS:

PC COMMIE FREAK FOOD

★ ALL-AMERICAN FREEDOM FOOD ★

SALE! LARD BALLS 50% OFF

CHECK OUT THAT TRAITOR BUYING AN ARTICHOKE.

GASP!

BROCCOLI 1.79/LB

AND THE CYCLE CONTINUES...

OKAY, FOLKS. HOW SHOULD WE MARKET OUR NEW **PORK BOMB SUPREME** DEEP-FRIED SAUSAGE PATTY WITH BACON AND CHEDDAR?

WE'VE GOT $20 MILLION TO WORK WITH.

BURGER POTENTATE

THERE'S ALWAYS, "IT'S THE TASTE SENSATION THE FOOD POLICE DON'T WANT YOU TO EAT!"

It's not just Burger King pushing the "PC food" meme. After I drew this cartoon, the *New York Times* ran an article about organic beef hot dogs, calling them "the politically correct frankfurter." It sounds like a harmless enough joke, but it really does reinforce the right-wing narrative that caring about the environment and our health is some sort of repressive form of snobbery. Also, speaking strictly from a humor standpoint, political correctness jokes are *so* 1992.

People Who Could Save the Day

Before the 2004 elections, it was tantalizing to think of all the nonvoters who could so easily rise up off their duffs and change the fate of the planet for the better. Sadly, they did not.

To be fair, turnout was relatively high in that election, but the reality-based voters were cancelled out by Swift Boat-tale swallowers.

After Bush triumphed in the 2004 election, I tried to console myself with the thought that I was not alone in my disappointment. I was, in fact, joined by half of America and the rest of the planet. The human race was on my side. Only a relatively small number of people had won. Unfortunately, they happened to control the most powerful nation on earth.

This cartoon was partly inspired by emails from Bush supporters who suggested I wasn't "open-minded" enough. I actually think the whole "who's more intolerant" debate is pretty silly, but alas, I will respond to my critics: Um, have you examined your own side lately? The one that demanded loyalty oaths at Bush rallies? The party of Bill "Shut up!" O'Reilly, Rush "feminazi" Limbaugh, Ann "faggot" Coulter, and Michael "die gay pig" Savage? Anyone who does not renounce all of these things up front before criticizing the left for being "intolerant" is not to be taken seriously.

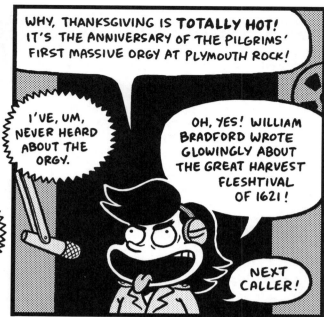

Pumpkin pie really is a powerful aphrodisiac. According to Dr. Alan Hirsch of the Smell and Taste Research Foundation, the scent of said pie, paired with lavender, increased penile blood flow in men by 40%. It also works on women, though a combination of cucumbers and Good & Plenty candy works best. Isn't science fun?

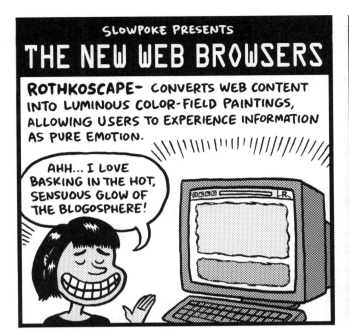

"Flaming Ferret" is, of course, a reference to Mozilla Firefox, the logo of which shows a fox curled around planet earth with its tail on fire. Or made of fire. I can't tell for sure.

It would be nice if television came with a BS blocker as well. There'd be an awful lot of dead air.

AND NOW IT'S TIME FOR THE

RECLAIMED LANGUAGE NEWS

THOUSANDS OF **PRO-LIFERS** MARCHED OUTSIDE THE WHITE HOUSE TODAY TO PROTEST THE WAR IN IRAQ.

100,000 INNOCENTS KILLED SO FAR

SUPPORT THE TROOPS-BRING 'EM HOME!

GET A CLUE

ALSO TODAY THE PRESIDENT CAUSED OUTRAGE IN THE **MORAL** COMMUNITY WITH A COMMENT ON HOUSING PROGRAMS FOR THE POOR.

WHO NEEDS SECTION 8 VOUCHERS WHEN YOU GOT THE GREAT OUTDOORS?

IN NORTHERN CALIFORNIA, A **DEFENDER OF TRADITION** WAS ARRESTED AFTER BLOCKING THE DESTRUCTION OF THE COUNTRY'S SOLE REMAINING NATIONAL FOREST.

HAVE YOU NO DECENCY, SIR?

Welcome to BIG OLD SEQUOIA NATIONAL PARK

SOON TO BE HALLIBURTON STADIUM!

AND FINALLY, A NUMBER OF **PATRIOTS** ARE CALLING FOR AN INVESTIGATION OF VOTING IRREGULARITIES IN OHIO AND FLORIDA.

WE'D GET A LOT FARTHER IF THE REPUBLICANS WOULD STOP THEIR **WHINING!**

PAPER TRAILS NOW!

COUNT EVERY VOTE

I would like to propose a moratorium on the terms "values voters" and "moral issues." These are nothing more than Big, Fat Right-wing Euphemisms, and the media seem perfectly happy to deploy them uncritically. Such language falsely implies that progressives don't have values and don't care about morality, and that morality itself is pretty much limited to the circumstances under which people can bump nasties. As opposed to, say, dooming thousands of people to premature death every month from air pollution.

HEY, DENIZENS OF THE HIGHWAY! HAVING TROUBLE KEEPING TRACK OF ALL THE LOOPY CAR DECALS OUT THERE? THEN IT SOUNDS LIKE YOU NEED...

The Field Guide to Magnetic Ribbons

 SUPPORT OUR TROOPS

 AS IF ANYONE DOESN'T

 I SUPPORT MAGNETIC RIBBON MANUFACTURERS IN CHINA

 I SUPPORT SOMETHING, BUT I FORGET WHAT

 MEMORIAL FOR LOST MAGNETIC RIBBON THAT FELL OFF CAR

 I LIKE CHEESE PUFFS

 CLOWN ON BOARD

HOLIER THAN THOU

 MY RIBBON CAN KICK YOUR RIBBON'S ASS

This is one of my most popular cartoons from the past few years. I wrote it on a train on the way back from a book tour through the Northeast with two other cartoonists. It was late March, 2005, and we'd spent a lot of time on highways behind cars plastered with magnetic "Support Our Troops" ribbons. Under normal circumstances, such displays wouldn't bother me, but given the context of these bizarre political times, in which opponents of the war are routinely tarred as unpatriotic, the ribbons strike me as sanctimonious and grating. I say this as someone who has a relative serving in Iraq. It's curious how, as the popularity of the war has declined, so has the ubiquitousness of the ribbons.

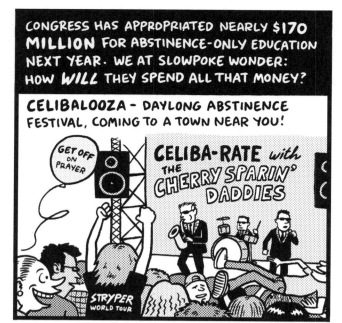

I love how Republicans squawk about social programs wasting taxpayer money, only to turn around and implement a big, honking social program—abstinence-only education—that has been clearly proven to waste taxpayer money. Abstinence-only education is crazy, unless you're for unwanted babies and genital warts. I have a hunch this is all just a sop to the genital wart cream industry (I hear they're big GOP donors).

This cartoon addresses an issue the Dems should be hitting hard: the fact that the Bush EPA has fought tooth and nail for years against meaningful controls on mercury pollution. Mercury is a powerful neurotoxin that collects in the bloodstream. Yet the "pro-life" party that insists on protecting stem cells apparently has no problem causing brain and nervous system damage to infants and children. In a rational world, this would be a huge political liability.

I think this strip in particular captures the sci-fi quality of our current national discourse.

As of this writing, at least one-fifth of the human genome has been patented. Not the physical genes in your body, but how those genes can be used by scientists. Critics say gene patenting stifles innovation by limiting who can perform research. The folly of "privatize-it-all" zealots is that they consistently see the owner's enrichment as benefiting the public, not taking something away. Some things, like health care and parks, should be accessible to all Americans, regardless of their point tally in the game of the marketplace.

What's In a Name?

WARNING: THERE'S A TRENDY NEW BABY NAME OUT THERE.

MEET **CASH**, OUR NEW BUNDLE OF JOY!

HE WAS JUST MINTED LAST MONDAY!

ÜRT?

(TRUE!)

COULD OTHER UPWARDLY-MOBILE NAMES BE FAR BEHIND?

BLING! TIME TO GO!

NASDAQ! MOMMY'S HERE!

COME, SUCCESS!

...OR CORPORATE SPONSORSHIP?

TOSTITO JUST LOVES HIS SALSA STROLLER!

LOOKS LIKE A CHIP OFF THE OLD BLOCK! HA! HA!

Tostitos CHUNKY-ST

LIPITOR 40mg

BEFORE LONG...

BOB?! WHO WOULD NAME THEIR KID BOB?!

WHAT A FREAK!

HI! I'M CUBICLE

HI! I'M IPOD

HI! I'M BOB

HI! I'M TOFURKEY

HI! I'M TEFLON

I received more angry email over this cartoon than any political strip I've ever done. The lesson here: don't mess with people's babies.

While visiting a posh resort area, I noticed two birth announcements in the local paper of babies named "Cash." It seemed like the latest step in name gentrification (see: Logan, Tyler, and Madison). But, as readers pointed out, Johnny Cash had died earlier that year, and Cash is also an old Anglo name, found in Faulkner's *As I Lay Dying*. Now, the people who named their baby Million'z A'Dolla'z have no such excuse. (I did not make that up.)

The fact that *anybody* took the Republicans' Social Security privatization scheme seriously explains the existence of cheesy late-night infomercials. (Did you know that you can make millions trading international currency from the comfort of your own home? YES! You can!) It occurred to me that these market fundamentalists are like dudes who refuse to use condoms, forcing unprotected capitalism on everyone.

Ever notice how frequently restaurants—especially steakhouses—play up themes of lawlessness? I've eaten at places called "Desperado's" and "Maverick." Perhaps the most famous example is the Republican-donor Outback Steakhouse, whose motto is "No rules, just right." (Or as Mr. Slowpoke says, "No rules, just wait to be seated.") Because rules suck, man. I cannot begin to count the times that rules have come between myself and a steaming platter of deep-fried onion wedges.

In case you couldn't tell from my "PC food" cartoon, one of my biggest pet peeves is the term "political correctness," a destructive, right-wing phrase that is parroted even by many socially-conscious types. It is a label loaded with bias, frequently applied with a broad brush to anything progressives stand for. In reality, right-wingers are masters of "political correctness": ridiculous euphemisms and denunciations of anyone who does not parrot their insane ideas. I find *this* political correctness, with its insistence on blind patriotism, to be far more pernicious.

What annoyed me most about this whole episode was not Summers's dunderheaded remark, but the common notion that his critics were being close-minded. The problem with the "inferior brain" explanation is that it ignores the overwhelming evidence of cultural biases—some overt, some subtle—that make the sciences seem more appealing to guys. It also ignores the history of gender in this country; my own university didn't even admit women until 1970! Deal with all that stuff, then get back to me with your sketchy sociobiology. This cartoon was featured in a management textbook, in a section that used Summers's speech as an example of what not to do.

TUBE SOCKS
Through the Years

1970s: GOLDEN AGE OF THE TUBE SOCK. THICK, TALL, FLUFFY, AND STRIPED, WITH EXCITING COLOR COMBINATIONS LIKE MUSTARD AND BROWN.

BEST WORN WITH REVEALING, CROTCH-LENGTH RUNNING SHORTS

1980s: STRIPES REPLACED BY SOLID COLORS, TYPICALLY PASTEL HUES INTENDED TO MATCH BENETTON SWEATSHIRT OF CHOICE.

benetton

FAT MATCHING SHOELACES A PLUS!

1990s–2000s: THE SHRINKING YEARS. PLAIN WHITE PREFERRED. GENTLY-SCRUNCHED SOCKS GRADUALLY REPLACED BY BARELY-THERE ANKLETS.

CONTROVERSIAL PAIRING OF SOCKS AND SANDALS CAUSES OUTRAGE IN SOME COMMUNITIES.

SOME RETRO-IRONIC TUBE SOCKS SPOTTED IN METROPOLITAN AREAS!

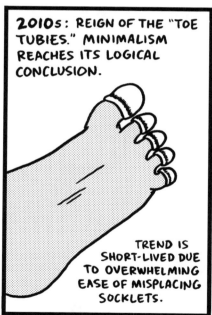

2010s: REIGN OF THE "TOE TUBIES." MINIMALISM REACHES ITS LOGICAL CONCLUSION.

TREND IS SHORT-LIVED DUE TO OVERWHELMING EASE OF MISPLACING SOCKLETS.

2015: RETURN OF THE POM-POM. SOCK ACCESSORIES ARE BACK... IN A BIG WAY!

THEN

NOW

2020: APPLE RELEASES THE iSOCK, THE WORLD'S FIRST DIGITAL-HOLOGRAPHY FOOTWEAR. USERS CAN DOWNLOAD DESIGNS FROM THE INTERNET AT 99¢ EACH!

I JUST FOUND THIS RARE ARGYLE SP3 ON SOCKSTER!

The line "Controversial pairing of socks and sandals causes outrage in some communities" was partly intended as an inside joke for readers of my local paper, the *C-VILLE Weekly*. The *C-VILLE* has a feature called "The Rant," in which readers call and leave messages about things they find irritating. For literally years now, people have been ranting about the fashion faux pas of stockinged feet in open-toed shoes.

After I drew this cartoon, I found out that Apple does in fact sell iPod socks, which are like cozies for your iPod.

As a member of the White House press corps, Jeff Gannon aroused suspicion for lobbing ridiculously supportive questions at Bush administration officials. He was eventually exposed as a fake reporter for a GOP propaganda website, and a male prostitute to boot. Laughably, Republicans accused those who questioned the propriety of this arrangement of homophobia.

In the spirit of academic inquiry, I conducted a thorough review of Gannon's escort-service websites, and can assure you he isn't missing any body parts.

I can understand the desire for ordinary rifles, but I fail to grasp the appeal of exotic firearms designed to turn bodies into gazpacho. I know titanium deer have been a problem in some parts of the country, but really, there are other ways of dealing with them.

The ponytailed gun dealer is loosely modeled after Ted Nugent.

MORE **SUBCULTURE WARRIORS**

BERNARD PIMBLE
DOES TAI CHI IN PUBLIC

MORTIMER PERKINS AND ERICA FUNKEN
DRESS THEIR OFFSPRING LIKE
MINIATURE VERSIONS OF THEMSELVES

CUSTOMER SERVICE

THIS TOASTER LEAVES MY BREAD SO PALE,
IT MAKES ME WANT TO SCREAM AND WAIL!
TAKE BACK THIS APPLIANCE OF DEFIANCE
AND UN-RELIANCE,
AND GIVE ME CASH
BEFORE I SMASH!

CLAUDIA VERBOSA
SPEAKS ONLY IN SLAM POETRY

Dear Mr. Wallbanger,
   Thank you for your letter. I could not disagree more vehemently. I will continue to support the execution of retarded grandmothers forever.

                    Sincerely yours,
                    Rep. Edwin Snoode

THOMAS WALLBANGER
PERSISTS IN WRITING HIS RED-STATE
CONGRESSMAN DESPITE INEVITABLE RESULTS

Every so often I draw a "Subculture Warriors" strip about people who doggedly insist on doing some unusual thing. This one began when I saw one of those tai chi guys blissfully executing forms in the middle of a grassy patch at the University of Virginia, mindless of the flow of students and traffic around him.

The last panel is based on my repeated experience writing my awful Republican congressman, only to receive a predictably disappointing form letter in return. The name "Edwin Snoode" is a play on Virgil Goode.

This cartoon grew out of my frustration at over-hyped media spectacles, particularly the Terri Schiavo case, in which Republican political opportunists descended in droves upon a poor brain-dead woman in Florida whose husband wished to remove her feeding tube. I was loath to address that tired story directly, so I broadened the topic to the GOP's media dominance. In a rare occurrence, the Schiavo gambit ultimately backfired on them.

The concept here was inspired by David Brock's book, *The Republican Noise Machine: Right-Wing Media and How It Corrupts Democracy*. Also, I like drawing silly machines.

A meme often spouted by Beltway blowhards is that the Dems simply don't have any "ideas." While the Dems in Congress do seem to have a problem articulating a coherent, unified message, that hardly means progressives don't have any thoughts about how to do things better. The problem is, most of the time we're too busy trying to stop the barrage of crap the Republicans keep throwing at us to outline some Lofty Vision of the Future. This was especially the case when I drew this cartoon, when the Dems were the minority party in the House and Senate.

I drew this not long after Joseph Ratzinger was anointed Pope Benedict XVI. As a cardinal, Ratzinger was especially active in trying to ban gay marriage around the world. I realize you can't expect the Pope to own the complete *Queer as Folk* on DVD, but given what was happening in the U.S., the timing was especially bad.

It's appalling how the puritanically correct in this country fixate on homosexuality to the exclusion of grave moral issues like the suffering of innocents in Iraq. I can only imagine any Supreme Being would be dismayed.

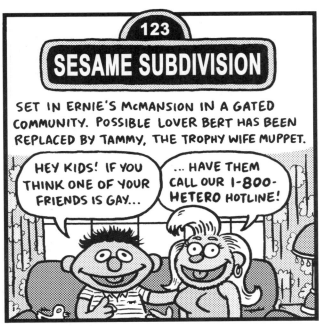

The chairman of the Corporation for Public Broadcasting, a Bush lackey, conducted a secret study of PBS's *NOW With Bill Moyers,* in which guests were placed into categories like "anti-Bush," "anti-business," and "anti-Tom Delay." Like so many other attempts to divide the world into "liberal" and "conservative," such categories completely ignore context. An exposé on, say, a chemical plant poisoning its employees is hardly anti-business, unless you think a business should be free to murder its workers. And as for Tom Delay, exactly how big a crook does someone have to be before we can call them a crook without being accused of partisanship?

HEY ASPIRING SCREENWRITERS! WANT TO CREATE A HOLLYWOOD HIT? JUST FOLLOW THIS HANDY GUIDE TO... **BLOCKBUSTER MOVIE FORMULAS!**

YE OLDE ACTION HERO GENDER-BENDER

HANS HAMMERLOCK IN

MEAN QUICHE

WHATEVER YOU DO, DON'T INSULT HIS QUICHE.

KISS THE COOK

A DOUBLE FEATURE WITH:

THOR
CHANGES DIAPERS

THE ODD COUPLE ROMANCE:
A TIMELESS CROWD-PLEASER!

SHE'S A PERKY CAREER GIRL. HE'S A GIANT DOG BISCUIT. CAN THEY MAKE IT WORK?

CHLOË CLICHÉ IN

MILKBONED

AND DON'T FORGET THE POP CULTURE COW— SHE'S NOT DRY YET! THERE'S STILL PLENTY LEFT TO DESTROY!

Kalvin and Hobbes
THE MOVIE

STARRING DANNY DEVITO, JULIA ROBERTS, TOBY TWITT AS KALVIN, AND THE VOICE OF ASHTON KUTCHER AS HOBBES!

THE RECYCLED CLASSIC
UPDATE AN OLD FAVE FOR THE 21ST CENTURY!

HERBIE THE LOVE HUMMER

= BEEP! = BEEP!

THE AGE 12-TO-16 MALE MARKET MOVIE

FROM FOCUS GROUP FILMS
THE BLAST

ONE 90-MINUTE LONG EXPLOSION!

Not long after I drew this, I found out they were indeed coming out with a new Herbie the Love Bug movie—*Herbie: Fully Loaded*—for the Generation Y audience. It's a truism among cartoonists these days that reality keeps eclipsing our attempts at satire.

Ever notice how odd-couple romances often pair an attractive woman and a dumpy guy she would never date in real life? If there were more women screenwriters, that wouldn't happen so much.

SOME PEOPLE BLAME NEWSWEEK'S BRIEF MENTION OF KORAN-FLUSHING FOR CAUSING VIOLENT, ANTI-AMERICAN PROTESTS IN SEVERAL MUSLIM NATIONS.

NEWSWEEK LIED PEOPLE DIED

WE WOULD NEVER FLUSH THEIR SILLY LITTLE BOOK DOWN THE TOILET.

IF THEY'RE RIGHT, IT WOULD BE ONE OF THE...

BLURBS THAT CHANGED THE WORLD

THE CIVIL WAR WAS CAUSED BY AN OBSCURE PARAGRAPH IN THE SATURDAY EVENING POST.

∞ NOTED ∞

North Carolina tobacco magnate Chester P. Calhoun was overheard last Thursday bragging about his new, custom-crafted Slave-Whip: "At one hundred-four inches long, with a fine-grain leather flayer, it is the greatest whip in all the Confederacy."

* * *

AFTER FIGHTING BROKE OUT, THE MAGAZINE RETRACTED THE PIECE, CITING UNCERTAINTY OVER WHETHER MR. CALHOUN SAID 104 INCHES OR 105. BUT IT WAS TOO LATE.

U.S. FORCES WERE WELL ON THEIR WAY TO A CLEAR AND DECISIVE VICTORY IN VIETNAM UNTIL THIS FUN FACT APPEARED IN THE JUNE 1967 ISSUE OF HIGHLIGHTS MAGAZINE.

Did You Know...?

It takes less than 22 minutes to incinerate an average Vietnamese peasant village.

PRACTICE MATH WITH
DENNY the
DIVISION DRAGON!

ANTIWAR PROTESTERS WERE AROUSED, AND IT WAS ALL DOWNHILL FROM THERE.

SOON: A CLASSIFIED AD IGNITES WORLD WAR THREE!

WANTED: Enriched uranium. Will pay top price. Discreet delivery method preferred. Contact K.J. Il, dearleader@ pyongyangnet.co.kp

FUTON - $40 OBO. Good condition. Call Mike, 873-

Newsweek printed a short news piece stating that American interrogators at Guantánamo had flushed a Koran down a toilet to demoralize detainees. The story made its way around the world, sparking violent protests in which several people were killed. Bush supporters lashed out at *Newsweek* for its negative portrayal of the U.S. war effort, and the magazine retracted the report. I thought it was funny how they blamed the riots on a little blip in a magazine *and nothing else*—like, oh, invading Muslim countries, humiliating prisoners at Abu Ghraib, and herding people into camps with no legal recourse.

Once upon a time, the U.S. government was distinct from the private sector. It seems almost quaint now, but elected officials actually tried to protect the public good and maintain a degree of ethics in the marketplace. Now, corruption is de riguer for even well-meaning politicians. If you ask me, the only way out of our current system of legalized bribery is with 100% publicly-financed elections. Compared to the Iraq War, this reform would cost nothing. And it might help us avoid such wars in the future.

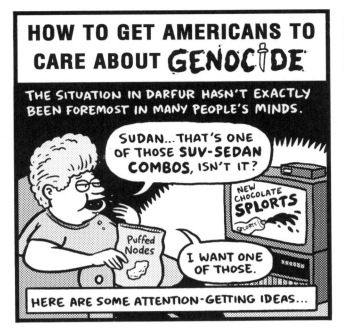

HOW TO GET AMERICANS TO CARE ABOUT GENOCIDE

Don't the faux-human rights activists who supported the "liberation" of Iraq look like two-faced weenies when it comes to Sudan? "Saddam gassed his own people!" they bellowed over and over, referring to the atrocious massacre of the Kurds in 1988. Well, we've had a real, live genocide happening for years, and where have those armchair liberators been? Such fickle freedom fighters they are. Rush Limbaugh even suggested that Democrats were only expressing concern about Sudan because they were currying favor with black voters. Yes, he did.

It must be nice to live in a world where the truth is whatever you want it to be. In addition to the former oil lobbyist's edits shown in the first panel, the Bush administration also watered down a 2005 G8 statement on global warming. One of the changes was the deletion of the opening statement, "Our world is warming."

Global warming is a perfect example of something often treated as a "liberal" issue, one side of a two-sided argument. But it's not, unless you're pro-drowning the people of Tuvalu.

TRUE: SOME COMMUNITIES, INCLUDING THE CARTOONIST'S, COLLECT TOXIC WASTE LIKE SOLVENTS AND PESTICIDES ONLY TWICE A YEAR (IF THAT).

SIGH.

CITY DUMP
HAZARDOUS WASTE COLLECTION MINUTE:
OCT. 12
9:00-9:01 AM

PAINT THINNER

SINCE MANY AMERICANS DON'T EVEN RETURN THEIR SHOPPING CARTS, THIS POLICY SEEMS OVERLY OPTIMISTIC.

FO#K THAT!

NO DUMPING
FLOWS TO WATERWAYS

POISON

WHY NOT SAVE A FEW MORE TAX DOLLARS WHILE WE'RE AT IT?

SORRY MA'AM, BUT WE ONLY ACCEPT CRIME REPORTS ON THE VERNAL AND AUTUMNAL EQUINOXES.

SANITATION DEPARTMENT, SIR. I'M AFRAID YOU'VE EXCEEDED THE CITY'S "TWO FLUSH PER ANNUM" LIMIT.

FINE

KIDS: COME UP WITH YOUR OWN COST-CUTTING, "BEAST-STARVING" IDEAS AND SEND 'EM TO YOUR ELECTED OFFICIALS!

I drew this cartoon while in the process of moving. I wanted to get rid of some nasty solvents and cleaners, most of which had accumulated from roommates at a prior house. One item was a can of Brasso brass polish from the '70s, if not earlier. But alas, my local facility only accepts most hazardous household waste for a few hours two days a year. If you manage to remember the magical dates, you still must drive the items several miles out of town. Woe to you if you don't own a car. Needless to say, that damned can of Brasso followed me to my new house.

While John Roberts was surely chosen for a number of reasons—his thin judicial record not the least of them—I do think the Bushies were aware that his golden-boy appearance would be good PR. Even many Democrats were duped into viewing him as a sort of "moderate" conservative. Beneath the attractive facade and genteel personality, however, lies a hideous, Borkish creature. His rulings since I drew this cartoon have neatly borne out my prediction that he would steer the court to the hard right.

THE NEW ENERGY BARS

HEY, CONSUMERS! EVER NOTICED THERE'S AN ENERGY BAR LIKE THIS ONE FOR ALMOST EVERY DEMOGRAPHIC?

LOONA URBAN NEW AGE GODDESS BAR

CHECK OUT THESE LATEST NICHE-MARKETED TREATS!

THE PRO-X3™ AMINO BOOSTER METABOLIC SYMMETRY CROSS-TRAINING TOTAL BODY BAR®
INGREDIENTS: PUFFED RICE, CHOCOLATE, SUGAR

IRONY BAR

BOLTON BAR
WITH RABID BADGER TO ENHANCE SURLINESS, AND VITAMIN B COMPLEXES FOR THICK, BUSHY MUSTACHE GROWTH

SLOTH BAR
FOR THOSE WHO SIT.

THE BOOM BAR
WITH BUILT-IN SUBWOOFERS, IT'S THE ONLY BAR WITH BLOCK-ROCKIN' BASS!

THE RNC™ POWER-HUNGRY BAR
IF YOU EAT ANOTHER BRAND, YOU'RE WITH THE TERRORISTS.

I actually find energy bars pretty handy, but the packaging is getting a little ridiculous. I'm not sure what rain forest iconography or Matisse cut-out women dancing in some sort of moon-worship ritual have to do with my need for a portable snack.

John Bolton was the firebrand neocon Bush forced upon the United Nations as the U.S. ambassador. His rather unkempt, hirsute appearance made him a pleasure to draw for many cartoonists, myself included (see also "Whack a Whackjob!" page 35).

I didn't have room to explain it well in the cartoon, but the lesson about the sun standing still in the sky was part of a course developed by a religious advocacy group called the National Council on Bible Curriculum. The council had succeeded in getting a Bible study course into schools under the guise of "historical" and "literary" study. But the teachings included proselytizing language and urban legends, such as one that NASA found evidence that the earth stopped twice in its orbit, as the Bible describes in Joshua and II Kings.

Not too long after the Iraq War began, I read an article that quoted a Hummer fan describing the behemoth SUV as "patriotic." I guess that's what counts as sacrifice for the war effort these days: driving an overpriced, gas-sucking monstrosity that resembles a military vehicle. I'm sure the troops appreciated this show of solidarity.

I like casting Hummer owners in the role usually occupied by people earnestly trying to save large ocean mammals.

TRUE: ASKED ABOUT ULTRACONSERVATIVE SUPREME COURT NOMINEE JOHN ROBERTS, RECENTLY-RETIRED DEMOCRATIC SENATOR JOHN BREAUX SAID THIS:

ROBERTS IS A GOOD FAMILY MAN WITH BEAUTIFUL CHILDREN.

YOU HAVE TO BE VERY CAREFUL ABOUT HOW YOU APPROACH DIGGING INTO THE BACKGROUND OF SOMEBODY WHO APPEARS TO BE A GOOD GUY.

HERE ARE MORE DEMOCRATIC SENATORS' COMMENTS ON UPCOMING ISSUES!

THE FDA RECOMMENDS THAT CHILDREN BE FORCE-FED FIVE POUNDS OF GROUND CHUCK DAILY.

WHY, I'M PRO-HAMBURGER, OF COURSE!

WE DON'T WANT TO WASTE OUR POLITICAL CAPITAL!

GLORK!

BUSH APPOINTS DAVID DUKE TO HEAD A NEW COMMITTEE ON RACE RELATIONS.

EH, WE'LL LET THIS ONE GO. WE DON'T WANT TO LOOK LIKE EXTREMISTS.

PLUS, I HEAR HE DRIVES A BOSS CAR!

A REPUBLICAN-SPONSORED BILL REQUIRES ALL DEMOCRATS TO WEAR BABOON SUITS.

IF YOU WANT TO GROW THE PARTY, YOU CAN'T ALWAYS PLEASE THE BASE!

OOO! OOO! OOO!

SO, SENATOR, WHAT WILL YOU DO WITH ALL YOUR POLITICAL CAPITAL?

RETIRE!

Breaux's quote in the first panel makes my point perfectly about the power of Roberts's image. He has beautiful children. He appears to be a good guy. Heaven forbid we require more of a judge on the highest court in the land! What gets me is that the Democrats constantly cave out of a misguided sense of caution, but to what end? Getting re-elected so they can continue caving? The Supreme Court is the Big Chalupa. If they won't fight for that, what is the point of holding office at all?

Breaux has since gone on to start a lobbying firm with former Republican Senator Trent Lott.

An interesting tidbit that ties into the last panel: in the wake of Katrina, market fundamentalist John Stossel argued that price gougers charging $20 for bottled water save lives by ensuring only those who need it most desperately will buy it. Stossel curiously sidestepped the problem of people desperately needing that $20 bottle of water but not being able to afford it. You know, having just lost everything they owned. Just a thought.

PRESIDENTIAL PHOTO-OPS MADE E-Z

1. Prepare

OKAY, GEORGE. WHEN YOU MEET THE VICTIMS, FURROW YOUR BROW. NO WINKING! THINK **SAD**. LIKE THE TIME THAT OIL WELL IN ABILENE TURNED UP **DRY**...

SNIFF!

2. Show compassion

I HAVE NOTHING LEFT!

DRY WELL... DRY WELL... DRY WELL...

HAVE YOU TRIED DRILLING ELSEWHERE?

I MEAN— I AM SO SORRY!

3. Bring 50 FEMA firefighters as props

UH SIR, WE REALLY SHOULD BE OUT RESCUING—

WAIT! THIS SHOT IS FOR THE WHITE HOUSE WEBSITE!

4. Joke about your partying days in New Orleans

I USED TO ENJOY MYSELF HERE, OCCASIONALLY **TOO MUCH!** HEH-HEH.

ONCE THERE WAS THIS HOT CHICK WHO HAD A MARGARITA GLASS STUCK BETWEEN HER TA-TA'S...

5. Joke about rebuilding Trent Lott's home

OH, THE NEW ONE'LL BE A **DOOZY!**

YEP.

6. Find scenes of inspiration

CAN YOU HOLD THAT POSE WHILE WE MOUSSE THE PRESIDENT'S HAIR?

Panels 3, 4, and 5 are based on real events. On the heels of a stoner-slow response from the federal government, Bush's trip to the Gulf was a PR disaster. Even at that late hour, he seemed clueless about the depth of the tragedy, and strangely unmoved. With untold numbers dead, and thousands of poor people newly homeless, the prez turned the spotlight on a wealthy Republican senator: "Out of the rubbles [sic] of Trent Lott's house—he's lost his entire house—there's going to be a fantastic house. And I'm looking forward to sitting on the porch." D'oh!

The reality was a bit more sinister than this cartoon. Under the guise of providing funding for Katrina victims, House Republicans proposed a 23-page list of government program cuts. The problem was, "Operation Offset," as it was called, amounted to little more than a partisan wet dream. The programs were ones they'd been trying to gut for years. Among their targets were Amtrak, Americorps, family planning, legal services for the poor, and of course the Corporation for Public Broadcasting. After all, PBS might actually report on how they were screwing us.

TO MAKE ENDS MEET, THE NY TIMES HAS BEGUN CHARGING $50 TO READ SOME OF THE COUNTRY'S BEST PROGRESSIVE COLUMNISTS ONLINE, AND IS TRYING TO TAKE THEM OUT OF PUBLIC SYNDICATION.

KRUGMAN

MEANWHILE, FOX NEWS GETS BUNDLED WITH BASIC CABLE WHETHER YOU WANT IT OR NOT.

I'D PAY $50 TO **BLOCK** THIS.

FOX

SOME PEOPLE DECIDE TO PROTEST...

PISSED OFF WITHOUT KRISTOF!

THE ONE GUY WHO READS THE TIMES FOR TIERNEY

HURTIN' FOR HERBERT

TIERNEY NOT TYRANNY

BUT THE **PROGRESSIVE SELECT™** PROGRAM IS EXPANDED.

...THANKS, MR. WILL. MR. HERBERT, WHAT'S **YOUR** VIEW?

REBUTTAL AVAILABLE TO SUBSCRIBERS ONLY!

AUTHORIZE $50 PAYMENT?

YES   NO

CNN

THE 2008 PRESIDENTIAL DEBATES:

IN CONCLUSION, MARTIAL LAW DESERVES A CHANCE.

YOUR *PROGRESSIVE SELECT™* ACCOUNT IS PAST DUE.

ACCESS DENIED

THANK YOU, MR. BUSH. MR. EDWARDS?

EVENTUALLY, THE PROTESTERS DWINDLE.

FREE KRUGMAN

WHO?

THANKS TO SJ

Astute readers will note that this strip does not fault the *New York Times* for trying to stay financially afloat; nor does it suggest that columnists should not get paid. I don't follow the philosophy that everything should be free, man (insert bubbling bong sound here). Here's the problem: right-wing pundits dominate today's major media. The last thing the country needs is for some of the most influential progressive voices to be even further marginalized. Fortunately, after two years, the *Times* ended "TimesSelect."

That's supposed to be Jeb Bush in the fifth panel. Yeah, that conjecture was a little off the mark.

This Week in CASUAL COUTURE

ONCE RELEGATED TO THE BARGAIN BINS, FLIP FLOPS NOW FETCH A PRETTY PENNY FROM GUCCI.

Sale!

TRADITIONAL FLIP-FLOPS: $1.99

Do not touch the shoe.

GUCCI THONG SANDALS: $325

HERE ARE SOME OTHER LOW-FASHION ITEMS GONE UPSCALE YOU MAY HAVE MISSED.

THE PRADA CHUGGER CAP— SPECIALLY-DESIGNED TO HOLD STEMMED GLASSWARE!

OLD SCHOOL

NOW

DOLCE & GABBANA "SEX" WATER WINGS

THEY'RE NOT JUST FOR KIDS ANYMORE! BLACK ITALIAN LEATHER WITH METAL LETTERING.

DON'T YOU WANT ME, BABY.

SEX SEX SEX

SEX SEX SEX

WARNING: WINGS DO NOT ACTUALLY FLOAT.

BE SURE TO ROUND OUT YOUR ENSEMBLE WITH THESE FINE ACCESSORIES!

LOUIS VUITTON NAVEL LINT

DON'T SETTLE FOR THE CHEAP FUZZ!

VERSACE BUBBLE BLING

VERSACE

LET EVERYONE KNOW YOU BLEW A WAD FOR THAT WAD!

SALVATORE FERRAGAMO DESIGNER DOG POOP
BECAUSE YOU MAY AS WELL STINK IN STYLE!

I continue to be fascinated by the flipflop trend. Back when I was a college lass, in ye olde grunge era, flipflops were reserved for the pool and the beach. Now flipflops are everywhere on college campuses, and they've gone posh. Gucci flipflops—okay, "thong sandals"—retail for over $300. Hence the premise of this strip, the extreme upscaling of "low" fashion.

The "sex" water wings in the third panel are based on a real belt from Dolce & Gabbana, which was covered with the word "SEX" and retailed for $185.99.

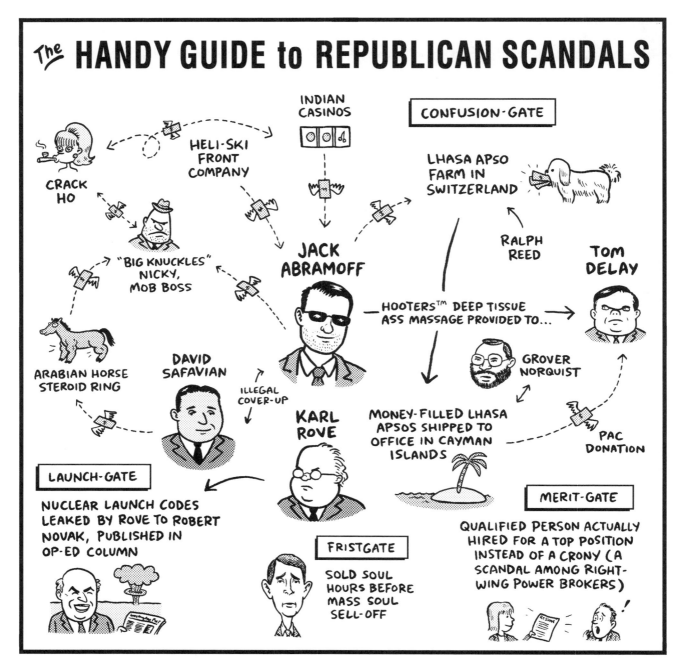

I drew this as the Jack Abramoff scandals were coming to light. Abramoff, to put it briefly, was a crooked lobbyist with close ties to many powerful Republican leaders; he was ultimately imprisoned on multiple felony counts. Others in his circle, including several public officials, were also convicted. The details of his corrupt dealings are so byzantine—involving Indian tribes, a floating casino, a golfing trip to Scotland, a mob-style murder, and more—that to this day I only have a tenuous grasp of what he did.

If a Democratic administration blew the cover of a CIA agent, as the Bush administration did with Valerie Plame, you know the right would be frothing at the mouth voluminously. Yet they sputtered all kinds of excuses for Plame's outing, such as that she wasn't really a covert agent (she was). The dearth of right-wing pundits willing to come forth and say, "Dude, that was uncool" was absolutely damning.

From the "Lipstick on a Pig" Files...

IN TYPICAL ORWELLIAN FASHION, THE RIGHT IS SPINNING VALERIE PLAME COVER-BLOWER KARL ROVE AS A VICTIM.

KARL ROVE, MALICIOUS? WELL, I NEVER!

THOSE NASTY DEMS! HOW LOW CAN THEY GO?

ONE CAN ONLY IMAGINE THESE FACT-TWIRLERS IN OTHER SITUATIONS...

GOLDFINGER WAS FRAMED. HE WASN'T TRYING TO DESTROY FORT KNOX— HE WAS TRYING TO SAVE IT!

THE LIBERALS JUST RESENT HIS LUST FOR GOLD.

JAMES BOND IS THE REAL ENEMY HERE!

BY BLOWING THE LITTLE PIGS' HOUSES DOWN, THE WOLF WAS ONLY TRYING TO ENCOURAGE THEM TO BUILD WITH STRONGER MATERIALS.

YES, THE REAL HUFFING AND PUFFING IS COMING FROM THE PIG COMMUNITY!

6#*!

MACHIAVELLI SAYS ETHICS SHOULD ALWAYS TRUMP POLITICAL GAIN!

UNLIKE THE LIBERALS!

The expression "Lipstick on a pig" seemed especially appropriate, given that Rove physically resembles a smooth, rounded oinker. And oh, does he squeal—on undercover CIA agents! While Richard Armitage was later found to be the source who leaked Plame's name to columnist Robert Novak, evidence pointed to Rove having an intimate hand in the affair, contradicting his earlier denials.

Regarding the last panel, some scholars say Machiavelli has been misunderstood—that *The Prince* was intended to be more descriptive than instructive. So comparing him to the swinish Rove may be unfair.

Paradoxes of Our Times

THE MINIMUM-WAGE OWNERSHIP SOCIETY

YOUR VERY OWN CAN OF LEGUMES IN SAUCE!

ONCE EMPTY, DOUBLES AS A CONTAINER FOR BEGGED CHANGE!

Beanie Weenies

CREDIT CARDS WITH **YOUR** NAME ON THEM!

BIGGIEBANK

YOUR OWN GRAVESITE (AFTER YOU EXPIRE EARLY DUE TO A LACK OF HEALTH INSURANCE)!

R.I.P.

STRIP MALL NOMENCLATURE

Ye Olde Village Centre EST. 1989

NAPPY Auto Parts   STARBORG'S COFFEE   BLOUSE BARN

SOCIALLY-CONSCIOUS TAILGATERS

EMBRACE DIVERSITY   LOVE YOUR MOTHER

OUTTA MY WAY, SCUMBAG!

THE "FREE" MARKET

FUNNY, I DON'T **FEEL** FREE...

YOU MISSED A CLOWN!

-SNAP!-

MINIATURE CLOWN NOSE ASSEMBLY STATION NO. 8

I'm not sure how Bush's "ownership society"—that fun-sounding euphemism for paying for everything from your health care to your retirement out of your own savings—is supposed to work if people don't earn enough to own anything.

The "strip mall nomenclature" panel was inspired by an actual strip mall I spotted along the highway in the outskirts of Washington, DC sprawl in northern Virginia. I believe it was actually called "Village Center." I assure you, it was anything but.

Legal Limericks
FEATURING SAMMY ALITO

There once was a judge named Alito
Who followed a radical credo.
He was named for the Court
After Bush's cohort
Received the party's veto.

His views – Oh, holy Toledo!
How he favors the power elite-o!
No new trial will be urged
If black jurists are purged,
According to Sammy Alito.

On choice he's decidedly weak.
Should it be an abortion you seek,
You must tell your spouse
Even if he's a louse;
The future of Roe sure looks bleak.

His backwards legal mind
Does not much like your kind.
He's Dobson's main man,
And he's just hit the fan –
Let's hope the Dems find their spine.

Oh, Alito. That lyrical name inspired me to draw the strip as a poem, even though there aren't really all that many words that rhyme with "Alito." You'd think there would be more. I thought about working in "Hirohito" but couldn't.

Alito has a plain, mushy face that's tricky to draw. For this strip I relied on some reference photos in which he appeared a bit chunkier than he is now.

"We do not torture." That's what Bush said at the same time Dick Cheney was seeking a torture exemption for the CIA. The statement was so brazenly false, it struck me as transcendent. It wasn't just an ordinary lie; it was an exercise in absurdity. The first thing that popped into my mind was Nixon's famous "I am not a crook" line, which I'm glad I managed to work into the strip. I can only hope this one goes down in history too, as one of the great whoppers of our times.

George's Thanksgiving

DEAR LORD, IT'S BEEN A TOUGH YEAR, BUT I'M STILL THANKFUL.

I'M THANKFUL FOR THE 37% OF AMERICA THAT WOULD CONTINUE TO SUPPORT ME EVEN IF I GAVE THE STATE OF THE UNION THROUGH MY BUTT CHEEKS LIKE THAT JIM CARREY FELLA.

I'M THANKFUL FOR "CLUBBY," MY FAVORITE 4-IRON, AND FOR THE COOL GRAPHICS IN MADDEN NFL 06... AND FOR JOE LIEBERMAN, WHO'S BEEN **SUCH** A SWELL GUY.

JOE, THIS DRUMSTICK'S FOR YOU!

CRACK!

I'M THANKFUL FOR "BLOSSOMIN' ONIONS" FROM THE AUSSIE STEAKHOUSE, FOR THE BITCHIN' PLASMA TV IN THE OVAL OFFICE, AND FOR A JOB WITH SO MUCH VACATION TIME.

ALSO, I'M THANKFUL I'M NOT INDICTED YET.

SAW! SAW! SAW!

SNAP! CRACK!

AND MOST OF ALL, I'M THANKFUL THAT MY **SUCCESSOR** WILL BE THE ONE TO PICK UP THE PIECES!

AMEN!

When George made a surprise visit to Iraq on Thanksgiving Day, 2003, he held aloft a plump, perfectly-dressed turkey as though he were serving it to the troops. The bird was, in fact, a decoration for the steam tables from which the troops got their actual chow. Many media outlets reported that the bird was plastic, hence the shattering turkey in this cartoon. I learned later that it was real, so my drawing is inaccurate. I apologize for the error. Lord knows no one needs to make stuff up about Bush to make him look like a boob. That the poultry was not plastic, of course, hardly changes the fact that the visit was an elaborately-staged photo op, or that justifications for the war turned out to be exactly as genuine as polyethylene fowl.

VIDEO GAMES ARE MORE LIFELIKE THAN
EVER THESE DAYS.

TOO MUCH INFORMATION BASEBALL

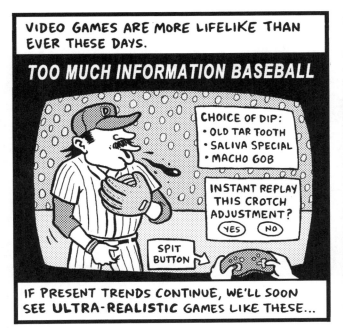

CHOICE OF DIP:
• OLD TAR TOOTH
• SALIVA SPECIAL
• MACHO GOB

INSTANT REPLAY
THIS CROTCH
ADJUSTMENT?
YES   NO

SPIT
BUTTON

IF PRESENT TRENDS CONTINUE, WE'LL SOON
SEE **ULTRA-REALISTIC** GAMES LIKE THESE...

STUCK BEHIND IDIOTS '06

YOUR MISSION: TO GET AROUND OBLIVIOUS
PEOPLE ON CELLPHONES ON A CROWDED
SIDEWALK.

LEVEL 3: SORORITY GIRL

SCORE
09

SO I WAS LIKE,
"THESE JELLO
SHOOTERS ROCK!"

ATTEMPT VERTICAL LEAP? YES NO

CLICHÉ COMBAT

GRAB A FRIEND AND GO HEAD-TO-HEAD
TRADING PLATITUDES AT A VIRTUAL
WATER COOLER!

FEELS LIKE IT
SHOULD BE FRIDAY.

CATCH THE BIG GAME?

I'VE STARTED THE ALL-
BEAN DIET.

COLD ENOUGH
FOR YA?

ANOTHER DAY,
ANOTHER DOLLAR.

MY CORNS HURT.

12   TRITE-O-METER   11

AND FANS OF GRAND THEFT AUTO WILL
LOVE **Xtreme JANJAWEED**

CHOP!

DUDE, THAT
DECAPITATION
WAS HARSH!

ALSO COMING SOON—**SECRET DETENTION
CENTER: ABOVE THE LAW**

Understanding Comics author Scott McCloud says we identify with stylized characters like Charlie Brown more than with photorealistic ones. I agree, especially when it comes to CGI animation and video games. Give me Mario and Luigi in the chunky, two-dimensional mushroom kingdom any day.

On top of the disturbing graphics, contemporary sports video games offer other real-life features like player endorsement and movie deals. Gag me with a joystick!

SINCE WE SEEM TO BE LIVING IN A NEW DARK AGE, PERHAPS IT'S TIME FOR...

A Marketing Plan for the ENLIGHTENMENT

THERE'D BE THE REASON BLIMP...

REASON FEVER— Catch it!

CELEBRITY ENDORSEMENTS...

I'M DROOLY JULIE. WHENEVER I'M DECIDING HOW TO PURSUE SOME BUFF YOUNG STUD, I USE **LOGIC!**™

PRODUCT PLACEMENT IN MOVIES...

DARLING, WHEN I SAW YOUR WIKIPEDIA ENTRY ON THE HORSEHEAD NEBULA, I KNEW I HAD TO HAVE YOU.

FAST FOOD TIE-INS...

HEY KIDS! TRY McSnottle's NEW **BILL NYE** the **SCIENCE GUY** HAPPY MEAL Featuring THE BIG BANG BURGER!

BOOM! BOOM! BOOM!

SCIENCE IS FUN!

...AND A NASCAR SPONSORSHIP!

THE **ENLIGHTENING ROD**

LOCKE
JEFFERSON
WOLLSTONECRAFT
BEN FRANKLIN
NEWTON

"Those who can make you believe absurdities can make you commit atrocities." —Voltaire

This is my plea for a more reality-based society. It may be the first cartoon in history to combine Mary Wollstonecraft and NASCAR racing. Her name is inscribed in tiny print on the side of the car; I wish I'd made it more legible. Wollstonecraft was an Enlightenment philosopher who argued for the rule of reason and the education of women, and against monarchy and slavery. Her "radical" views earned her the epithet "a hyena in petticoats," most likely from an ancestor of Bill O'Reilly.

This strip marks the debut of Mrs. Perkins. For some reason, it seemed imperative to me that she look vaguely Jetson-like. The two of them together remind me a little of myself and Mr. Slowpoke, although neither of us is dolicephalic.

The starting point for this one was the Paris Hilton Tinkerbell Gift Set, which I spotted in a department store while Christmas shopping. The little stuffed dog and bottle of eau de Paris were retailing for fifty bucks—a bit steep, I thought.

This strip refers to the "War on Christmas," the rabble-rousing myth Fox News perpetuates every year, condemning those who dare to wish someone "Happy Holidays" instead of "Merry Christmas." This is another subject I had planned to avoid doing a cartoon about because it annoyed me so much. Interpreting a small effort to be inclusive of, say, Jews celebrating Hanukkah as a declaration of war on Christianity is simply the height of *chutzpah*.

This basic misconception is at the root of so many problems with our political discourse. I can't tell you how many times I've heard from people who think I'm an "America hater" because I criticize the Bush administration. These same people, I'm sure, hardly perceived criticism of Bill Clinton's presidency as an attack on the country itself. I guess mocking the guv'ment is acceptable only when Democrats are in the White House.

WORDS Speak Louder than Actions

A CONTROVERSIAL JUDGE HAS BEEN NOMINATED TO THE SUPREME COURT.

JUDGE WACKITO, WE HAVE SOME CONCERNS ABOUT YOUR INVOLVEMENT IN THE ANIMAL SACRIFICE CLUB AT PRINCETON.

I CANNOT RECALL BEING A MEMBER OF THAT GROUP... BUT IF I WAS, IT WAS ONLY BECAUSE THE BIRDWATCHING CLUB WAS SHUT DOWN.

BUT IN 1985, YOU CLEARLY STATED, "KILL ALL THE CHIPMUNKS," AND YOU'VE REPEATEDLY DEFENDED CAT MUMMIFICATION.

I WAS ONLY DOING MY JOB AS AN ATTORNEY FOR THE RITUAL OFFERING LEAGUE OF AMERICA!

MOREOVER, I WOULD REFER YOU TO THE CASE OF CHIP AND DALE V. ACME TAXIDERMY FOR LEGAL PRECEDENT.

LATER, THE MEDIA ANALYSIS BEGINS.

THE DEMOCRATS COULDN'T LAY A FINGER ON WACKITO TODAY, JIM!

HE SURE KEPT HIS COOL WHEN ASKED ABOUT THE GOAT SARCOPHAGUS IN HIS BASEMENT!

I'D SAY HE'S QUALIFIED!

The Animal Sacrifice Club is a thinly-veiled reference to Samuel Alito's membership in a group called Concerned Alumni of Princeton, which opposed admitting women and minorities into the university. Alito touted his affiliation with the group on a 1985 job application with the Reagan administration. This alone should have posed a huge problem for his nomination to the Supreme Court, but his hearings proved that a nutty record can be overcome by merely maintaining one's composure. Infantile cable news "analysis" framed the Democrats' questions as partisan grandstanding, largely ignoring the substance of the concerns they brought up.

This cartoon came out of my repeated experience of enjoying a snowy trail in the wilderness out West, only to have the peace and quiet utterly destroyed by snowmobilers. (I am convinced there is a special circle in hell filled with nothing but snowmobiles and leaf blowers.) I was not imposing on the snowmobilers, but they were clearly ruining the experience for everyone on the trail, thus illustrating the concept that freedom does not exist in a vacuum. There's often a "freedom from" that is the flip side of "freedom to." Isaiah Berlin wrote about this in his famous essay, "Two Concepts of Liberty." In an age when the word "freedom" is so abused, its double-edged nature is important to remember.

Granted, the Dems won narrow majorities in the House and Senate in 2006 after I drew this, but I'd say those victories were in spite of their milquetoast waffling, not because of it. They were elected to end the war. Unbelievably, some Democrats still insist that the party hasn't been "centrist" enough. If these people were mice in a Skinner Box, no amount of electric zapping would deter them from going after the cheese the same way.

Meanwhile, since losing their majority, the Republicans have been whipping out filibusters right and left. Funny how they've suddenly shut up about obstructionism.

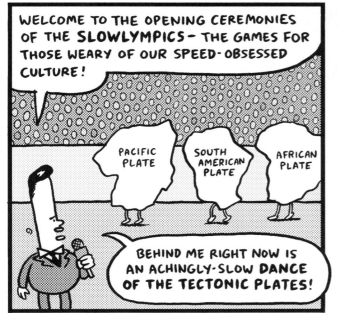

I drew this during the 2006 Winter Olympics. Except for the melodramatic horror show that is ice dancing, I enjoy watching the winter games. I like the fact that for two weeks, the living rooms of America are filled with obscure Nordic sporting events featuring athletes with names like "Roar." (See Roar Ljoekelsoey, ski jumping.)

The *Finnegans Wake* reference is a nod to my grandmother-in-law, an avid Joyce fan who spent several years dissecting that novel.

THE RUSH RIOTS OF '06

SOMEWHERE IN GEORGIA: A FARMER GROWS A FREAK EGGPLANT THAT RESEMBLES GEDDY LEE OF THE BAND RUSH.

SOMEONE ON AN INDIE ROCK MESSAGE BOARD MOCKINGLY POSTS A PHOTO OF THE EGGPLANT.

Malkmus1: Check out this eggplant that looks like Geddy Lee!

BeeThousand: Rush SUX!!

RahBras9: HA!

A COUPLE OF DIEHARD RUSH FANS SEE THE POST AND ARE INCENSED.

THIS IS AN INSULT TO **ALL OF RUSHDOM!**

HOW **DARE** THEY BLASPHEME "RED BARCHETTA" AND "FREE WILL"?

AFTER DOCTORING THE PHOTO TO MAKE THE EGGPLANT LOOK ROTTEN, THE TWO GO ON TOUR TO STIR UP ANGER AMONG RUSH FANS.

LOOK AT WHAT THESE PRETENTIOUS INDIE ROCKERS HAVE DONE TO THE **GOD OF THE BASS GUITAR!**

IT'S AN INSULT TO ALL CANADIANS!

THE MEDIA PICK UP ON THE STORY AND SPREAD THE IMAGE OF THE EGGPLANT AROUND THE GLOBE.

RUSH FANS PROTEST VEGGIE LEE

BBC

ANGRY PROG ROCKERS AND CANADIAN NATIONALISTS DESCEND ON HIPSTER MUSIC VENUES WITH TORCHES.

The Irony Bar

NEXT WEEK: A Q-TIP CAUSES NUCLEAR ARMAGEDDON!

This was my take on the Danish cartoon controversy, in which a newspaper provocatively printed a dozen cartoons of the prophet Muhammad, leading to violent Muslim protests and threats on the cartoonists' lives. While the comic is mostly silly, I did try to work in the point that the riots were more of a media-driven phenomenon than anything.

I heard from lots of Rush fans about this one, and was relieved to find they had a sense of humor. One of them issued a tongue-in-cheek fatwah, complaining that I had unfairly spared other prog acts like Styx, Yes, and Genesis. Sorry about that.

THE WEEK AFTER CHENEY'S HUNTING ACCIDENT, TIME MAGAZINE RAN A COVER STORY ABOUT HIS **RESOLUTENESS** TO DO THINGS HIS WAY.

STICKING TO HIS GUNS! WOO!

TIME

STICKING TO HIS GUNS

W
THE PRESIDENT

GIVEN THIS TENDENCY TOWARDS SPIN-AFFIRMING EUPHEMISMS, WHAT COVERS CAN WE EXPECT TO SEE IN THE FUTURE?

STORY: BUSH CHOKES ON SAMOSA WHILE IN INDIA. HEIMLICH PERFORMED, SAMOSA EJECTED ONTO PRIME MINISTER SINGH

KAFF!

AS REPORTED:

TIME
STRAIGHT SHOOTER
Behind Bush's Indian Diplomacy

STORY: CHENEY'S PANTS DROP DURING VISIT TO MILITARY BASE

AS REPORTED:

TIME
NAKED COURAGE:
Flanked by soldiers, Cheney's flanks soldier on

STORY: LAURA BUSH'S DOG MISS BEAZLEY GETS INTO SITUATION ROOM AND LAUNCHES ICBM AT FINLAND

REALLY LAUNCH MISSILE?
YES NO

AS REPORTED:

TIME
THE DOGS OF WAR
Even Bush's pets are unafraid to use force

Mr. Slowpoke and I got a big laugh out of this *Time* magazine cover when we saw it in a grocery store. We chuckled the entire way down the cereal aisle. Then, somewhere past the Honey Bunches of Oats, dismay set in. Even when Cheney accidentally shoots his friend in the face, our media use the incident to make him sound tough. Karl Rove could not have scripted it better. While the article itself adopted a less pandering tone, it was filled with personality-oriented psychobabble, such as the suggestion that Cheney was more "male" and Bush more "female." And we wonder why our democracy is failing.

SOUTH DAKOTA STATE SENATOR BILL NAPOLI EXPLAINS A POTENTIAL EXCEPTION TO THE STATE'S NEAR-TOTAL ABORTION BAN

A REAL-LIFE DESCRIPTION TO ME WOULD BE A RAPE VICTIM, BRUTALLY RAPED, SAVAGED. THE GIRL WAS A VIRGIN. SHE WAS RELIGIOUS. SHE PLANNED ON SAVING HER VIRGINITY UNTIL SHE WAS MARRIED.

THAT GIRL COULD BE SO MESSED UP... THAT CARRYING THAT CHILD COULD VERY WELL THREATEN HER LIFE.

(ACTUAL QUOTE)

SOON: AN ABORTION COURT IS ESTABLISHED TO DETERMINE WHICH SEXUAL ASSAULT VICTIMS GET THE EXCEPTION.

HMM... MISS KATZ, I GATHER YOU WERE ONLY GENTLY RAPED, AND THAT YOU OWN "BLACK SABBATH VOLUME 4."

I HEAR CRIBS ARE ON SALE AT WAL-MART.

THE STATE LEGISLATURE PASSES A BILL LISTING SOME EXCEPTIONS TO THE BAN.

A rape victim may seek an abortion in the following cases:
- She has been impregnated by a secular humanist
- She belongs to the Society for the Repression of Natural Urges
- She is a tender young milkmaid

But NOT if:
- She has hairy armpits
- She has read Erica Jong

EVENTUALLY...

SIOUX FALLS CITY HALL
Atheists and Fornicators Please Use Side Entrance

VIRGIN PARKING ONLY

Space limitations unfortunately caused me to leave out Napoli's additional words, "She was brutalized and raped, sodomized as bad as you can possibly make it, and is impregnated." I suspect that Mr. Napoli needed a cold shower after the interview. Over-the-top statements like this from politicians are God's gift to cartoonists.

South Dakota voters overturned the abortion ban in 2006.

Maladies of the INFORMATION AGE

GOOGLITIS — FRUSTRATION THAT ONE'S IMMEDIATE SURROUNDINGS ARE NOT INSTANTLY SEARCHABLE*

???

DAMN THE THIRD DIMENSION!

*YET.

ARCHIVAHOLISM

MY NAME IS JILL, AND I HAVE AN ARCHIVING PROBLEM.

I HOPE YOU DON'T MIND THAT I'M MAKING AN MP3 OF THIS DISCUSSION FOR POSTERITY.

ARCHIVAHOLICS ANONYMOUS

COMPULSIVE NEWS BINGING

REFRESH! REFRESH!

REFRESH! REFRESH! REFRESH!

REFRESH! REFRESH!

The Daily Luxembourgian

The Cape Horn Trumpeter

ENDLESS BABBLEBLOG

NEED... MORE... NEWS...

METAMANIA

MY SITE REVIEWS THE BEST SITES THAT FILTER SITES THAT PICK UP RSS FEEDS FROM SITES ABOUT GOURD POTTERY.

MY SITE RATES SITES LIKE YOURS!

I sometimes experience a vague sense of frustration that I cannot simply hit CTRL+F to find keywords in books. That was the seed behind the Googlitis panel of this cartoon, though a post-cartoon Google search revealed others have had similar ideas before me. It's hard to stay ahead of the geek curve. (As if to prove my point, a quick Google search reveals 92 instances of "geek curve.")

I know it's my job to find humor in the gradual destruction of America as we know it, but I sometimes reach a point where I am so repulsed by the Bushies, and so exasperated by the Democrats, that I can hardly stand to draw cartoons about them. So I drew a cartoon about being sick of politics. Yes, even we cartoonists get discouraged.

It's weird how most people don't want poison in their food, yet many scoff at organic edibles. I will be the first to admit that there's plenty of BS marketing out there—no one really needs hemp-infused loofah mousse (except, perhaps, Bill O'Reilly)—and organic food can be expensive. But people are quick to reject a label they don't identify with, even if this means contradicting their own rational beliefs. This is how politics works in the age of right-wing media domination: invoke a powerful stereotype, preferably in the form of a carefully-crafted sound bite, and people forget to think.

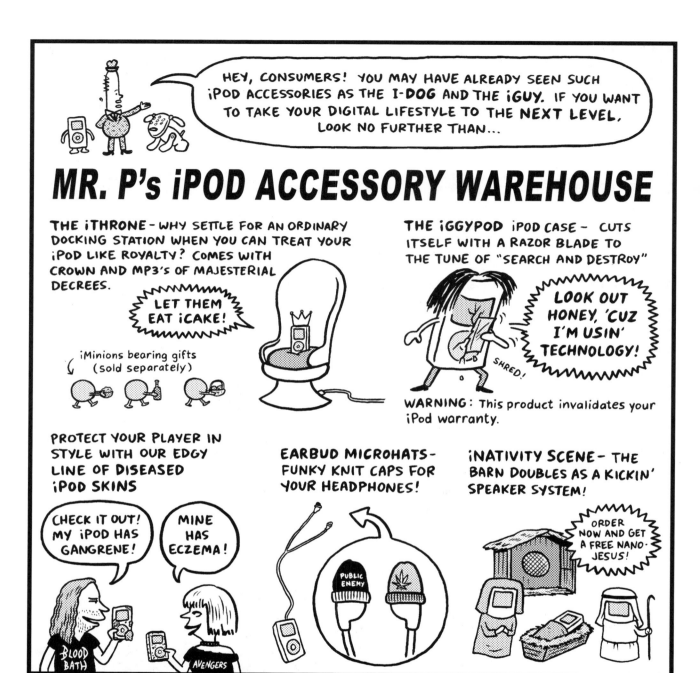

Did you know that Hasbro makes an "I-DOG" that dances to your MP3s? There's also the iKitty, a rubber, cat-shaped iPod protector, and the XtremeMac iBling, a kit for affixing hundreds of colored crystals to a snap-on iPod cover. Retails for only $40!

If I were a Sudanese refugee who spent my days eating dirt and fleeing decapitators, I would take great comfort in knowing that the Americans were spending hours on end gluing shiny stones to their portable music players.

AFTER YEARS OF LOBBYING BY THE FOOD INDUSTRY, THE HOUSE RECENTLY PASSED THE **NATIONAL UNIFORMITY FOR FOOD ACT** WHICH NEGATES STATES' FOOD SAFETY LAWS IN FAVOR OF WEAKER FEDERAL REGULATION.

WARNING: This food contains a chemical known to the State of California to cause cancer.

WHAT OTHER *NEW FOOD SAFETY LAWS* LIE AHEAD?

NUTRITION LABEL REFORM— RELAXES BURDENSOME ACCURACY REQUIREMENTS

I CAN'T BELIEVE THESE ONLY CONTAIN **ONE GRAM OF FAT!**

TALLOW TWISTS
ROCKIN' JALAPEÑO FLAVOR
HEART-HEALTHY!

THE PRETTY PRODUCE ACT—
AIRBRUSHED FRUIT LEGALIZED

Nature's Bosom
B A N A N A S

IN THE AGE OF PHOTOSHOP, PEOPLE DEMAND PERFECTION! WHY NOT GIVE IT TO THEM?

PSSSHT!

EVENTUALLY, LABELING IS NO LONGER AN ISSUE, AS THE FOOD INDUSTRY CONVINCES PEOPLE TOXINS ARE GOOD FOR THEM.

NEW **MERCULOIDS!** MOUNTAINS OF MMM-MMM- METHYLMERCURY IN EVERY BITE!

MOMMY! I WANT MERCULOIDS! I WANT MERCULOIDS!

YES, DEAR.

THANKS, SJ

For years Big Food has been pushing for the end of state regulation of labeling in favor of a uniform federal standard. Sounds reasonable in the abstract, right? The trouble is, the FDA *sucks*. States have long led the way in informing the public about food safety.

In another instance, the House banned states from labeling meat that has been injected with carbon monoxide to keep it artificially fresh-looking. This hotly-debated treatment causes beef to retain its blood-red color even after it has spoiled. The airbrushed bananas gag loosely alludes to this practice.

ᴏ⊙ Spectacle Semiotics: ⊙ᴏ
A RECENT HISTORY

1970s: HEYDAY OF ENORMOUS EYEWEAR

 MILES DAVIS' COSMICALLY-CHUNKY PLASTIC OCTAGONS

 MASSIVE BROWN FRAMES EMBODY "WHOLE EARTH, WHOLE FACE" PHILOSOPHY

 RETIRED-GUY-WITH-A-BOAT GLASSES

1980s: ERA OF ROUNDNESS

 LARGE, THIN FRAMES WORN BY ANDROGYNOUS NEW WAVERS

 EMERGENCE OF RIGHT-WING PUNDIT TORTOISESHELLS

 UN-CHANGED

1990s-2000s: SHRINKAGE!

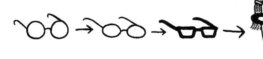

NEO-SCHOOLMARMISM

AS SMALL GLASSES GO BOURGEOIS, HIPSTERS RESORT TO IRONICALLY-HUGE FRAMES TO DIFFER-ENTIATE SELVES...

...LOOKING MORE AND MORE LIKE:

WHAT'S NEXT?

 MONOCLES APPEAR AMONG BOHEMIAN SET, 2009

 ON THE STREETS OF PARIS, 2022

 STILL AROUND, 2031

I'd been wanting to make fun of right-wing pundit glasses for quite some time, and this cartoon finally gave me the opportunity. You know the style: the round, slightly horn-rimmed, ultra-preppy look sported by the likes of George Will, Fred Barnes, and others. It's like they're trying to be old-school bankers or something.

I'm also fascinated by the contemporary revival of giant 1970s and '80s sunglasses. What began as an ironic statement is now everywhere, having spread to mall-cruising teenyboppers throughout the land. It's kind of weird for those of us who remember them from the first time around.

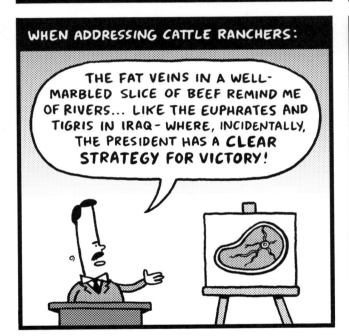

Yes, it's true: Department of Agriculture employees were actually asked to praise Bush's Iraq policy in their speeches. One of the main talking points USDA staffers were asked to mention was that Bush has a "clear strategy for victory in Iraq." (Bet you couldn't have guessed.)

I fear I have maligned manure with this strip. I have fond memories of catching earthy whiffs of the stuff as a youngster growing up in Pennsylvania. Perhaps "fond" is too strong a word. But I'll take meadow muffins over Bush administration policy any day.

Telecom companies want to prioritize internet delivery based on whether a site pays them fees or not. As you might imagine, this would end the democratic nature of the web. Whoever controls the flow of information defines reality, and that's why "net neutrality," like campaign finance reform, is a meta-issue that has bearing on all other issues. The telecoms ask, "Who should control the future of the internet? The government or the people?" That's funny; I thought that in a democracy, the government *was* the voice of the people. It's a classic Republican maneuver: redefining massive global conglomerates as YOU.

This is one of my personal faves. I had been toying around with the idea of what comes after our present age of extreme irony, which led to the panel about post-ironic cutism. Just a few weeks after drawing this, an artist friend introduced me to the site cuteoverload.com, which led me to ponder whether the age of post-ironic cutism was already upon us.

This cartoon is a sequel to one I drew in 2004 called "Gay Ban" about a spray that makes people focus on gay marriage instead of Bush's failings. My intent here is not to oppose discussion of immigration policy, but to address the race-baiting role it now plays in political campaigns. By the way, isn't it curious how the people complaining about the social ills caused by "the illegals" are mostly mum about the same problems—the loss of jobs, lowering of wages, and increased burdens on public infrastructure—caused by Wal-Mart?

See the Bonus Materials at the end of this book to find out why this cartoon was banned from a Texas prison!

I've observed a recurring trend in filmmaking: overwhelming attention paid to visual details like retro fashions and kitschy decor, accompanied by the total absence of meaningful plot. It's as though MTV has attenuated an entire generation's higher brain functions. I am especially weary of gratuitous ninjas and ironic mustaches. Note to Hollywood: these things do not equal automatic cool.

I actually saw an ad for *Borat* that consisted only of text written across his big, bushy you-know-what.

I wrote part of this cartoon while sitting in a local coffee shop that often displays the work of local artists. Directly in front of me were what appeared to be several large, blue, *papier-mâché* vulvas. I found them disturbing, yet somehow appropriate to the task at hand.

If anybody thinks I'm disrespecting the military with this cartoon, let me just say I have heard from The Troops. And they seem to like Drooly Julie.

Privacy Funnies

IN A BLOW TO PRIVACY RIGHTS, THE SUPREME COURT JUST OVERTURNED A CENTURIES-OLD PRECEDENT THAT POLICE OFFICERS MUST "KNOCK AND ANNOUNCE" BEFORE ENTERING A HOME.

MEANWHILE, IN A SOP TO THE GUN LOBBY, CONGRESS WANTS TO MAKE IT A FELONY FOR POLICE OFFICERS TO SHARE INFO ABOUT ILLICIT ARMS DEALERS.

SO... WE'RE PROTECTING THE PRIVACY OF KNOWN CRIMINALS WHILE WE INVADE THE PRIVACY OF SUSPECTS.

OF COURSE, THIS WOULDN'T BE THE FIRST TIME...

As if all of that government snooping and spying and wiretapping and data mining wasn't enough, Bush's two Supreme Court appointees did a little activist judgin', weakening a longstanding precedent stating that cops can't burst into your home without knocking. In *Hudson v. Michigan*, the winger majority deemed that evidence collected in violation of the rule is permissible in court.

The idiotic "Firearms Corrections and Improvements Act," which would have limited communication between police officers from different jurisdictions, fortunately never made it into law.

The law rejected by the Supreme Court limited how much a candidate could contribute to his or her own campaign. The Court cited the precedent of *Buckley v. Valeo*, which states that because speech often costs money, campaign money should be treated like speech. Uh-huh. (*Buckley* did uphold limits on individual contributions, to the consternation of money-equals-speech purists like Antonin Scalia.)

I think the strip wound up being a nice metaphor for how many aspects of life actually work in this country, including health care, as one reader suggested.

SELF-SERVE NATION

GROCERY STORES HAVE BEEN REPLACING CASHIERS WITH MACHINES, EFFECTIVELY OUTSOURCING LABOR ONTO CONSUMERS.

PLEASE PLACE YOUR ITEM IN THE BAG!

I DID, YOU IDIOT.

PLEASE PLACE YOUR ITEM IN THE BAG!

PLACE YOUR ITEM IN THE BAG NOW!

U-WORK

WHAT OTHER LABOR-FOISTING SCHEMES MIGHT LIE AHEAD?

SHOPPERS SENT TO SWEATSHOPS TO MAKE THEIR OWN APPAREL

DO YOU WANT AFFORDABLE CLOTHING OR NOT?

TOXI-GLU

TECH SUPPORT OUTSOURCED TO YOUR PARALLEL UNIVERSE SELF

...SO I NEED A FOUR-PIN MOLEX ADAPTER?

I HAVE NO FREAKIN' CLUE.

PERHAPS IT'S TIME TO FORM A CONSUMER LABOR UNION.

SHOPPERS LOCAL 729 ON STRIKE!

ÜBERFOOD SUPERMARKET

S.L. 729

I WON'T SCAN FOR THE MAN

NO PAY NO WEIGH!

I really hate automated checkouts. Mr. Slowpoke and I were forced to go through one of these bastard lanes because we were shopping late at night, and the store literally had no human cashiers on duty. Among our purchases were two ears of corn. I swear, to simply locate "corn" on the computer was like something out of the movie *Brazil*.

Not only are these devices usurping working-class jobs, but they create stressful work for the employee charged with overseeing many of them at once. Simply put, this person is often yelled at. As a former grocery store cashier, I implore you not to U-Scan!

During the 2006 Senatorial races, a popular line among establishment pundits was that progressives knee-jerkily opposed anyone who supported the Iraq War. As if that's the only reason we tried to get rid of Lieberman! Among other things, he voted for cloture on the Alito nomination, his wife worked for a major pharmaceutical lobbying firm, and he led the fight in 1994 against expensing stock options on corporate balance sheets, thus paving the way for accounting scandals. Not exactly a man of the people, that Joe.

Trading Places

THE SENATE RECENTLY PASSED THE "CHILD CUSTODY PROTECTION ACT," CRIMINALIZING THOSE WHO HELP A MINOR CROSS STATE LINES TO GET AN ABORTION WITHOUT PARENTAL CONSENT.

...BECAUSE EVERYONE LIVES IN A NICE NUCLEAR FAMILY WHERE PARENTS KNOW BEST!

WE HEREBY PROPOSE A NEW BILL — THE INANE LAWMAKER RESTRICTION ACT — WHICH IMPEDES SENATORS WHO VOTED FOR THE ABORTION BILL FROM LEAVING THEIR HOME STATES.

BUT — BUT — I'M JUST HIS PILOT!

TELL IT TO THE JUDGE, HON.

BEFORE LEAVING FOR D.C., THE SENATORS MUST OBTAIN CONSENT FROM A GROUP OF ABUSIVE, ALCOHOLIC, MENTALLY-ILL, DRUG-ADDICTED PARENTS.

IF YOU COULD JUST SIGN HERE, I'LL BE ON MY WAY, HEH-HEH!

LIKE HELL YOU WILL!

SO I HEARD YOU VOTED AGAINST RAISING THE MINIMUM WAGE!

IS THAT A ROLEX?

IT'S ALL PART OF A NEW, ABSTINENCE-ONLY POLICY!

IF YOU DON'T KNOW THE SOCIAL EFFECTS OF THE LAWS YOU'RE PASSING, NOT DRAFTING THEM AT ALL IS THE SAFEST CHOICE!

I had a feeling somebody would misinterpret this as saying that all anti-abortion parents are abusive, alcoholic, mentally-ill drug addicts. Sure enough, an incensed reader wrote to say I had demeaned millions of decent American families. Let me be clear: I am not in any way suggesting that all parents opposed to abortion are, as Axl Rose might say, on the Night Train. Nor are they loaded like a freight train, or flyin' like an aeroplane, or speedin' like a space brain one more time tonight. I am simply arguing that a teenage girl should not be forced to seek permission from a messed-up parent.

NEW SATELLITE RADIO CHANNELS

WITH PROGRAMMING BECOMING EVER MORE SPECIFIC, THERE'S NOW A STATION FOR EVERYONE!

THE RINGTONE CHANNEL

BLEEDLE-BLEEDLE
BLEE-DLE
BLEEEE-DLE!

PLAY THAT FUNKY MUSIC WHITE BOY

THE OB-LA-DI CHANNEL

ONLY PLAYS THE CHORUS TO THE BEATLES' "OB-LA-DI" *

OB-LA-DI!
OB-LA-DA!

OB-LA-DI!
OB-LA-DA!

* NOT TO BE CONFUSED WITH THE NA-NA-NA-NA-NA-NA-NA CHANNEL WHICH ONLY PLAYS THE CODA TO "HEY JUDE"

DUELING ZITHERS CHANNEL

PLINKA
PLINKA
PLINK
PLINK
PLINK

NEW AMBIENT STATIONS!

CHOMP!

THE PRETZEL-CRUNCHING CHANNEL

QWERT! QWERT!

THE HAND FART CHANNEL

WHAP!

OOH!

THE PLAYFUL ASS-SLAPPING CHANNEL

THE TALK BOX CHANNEL

FANS OF PETER FRAMPTON WILL LOVE IT!

DO YOU FEEL LIKE I DO?

HACKNEYED JAZZ STANDARDS CHANNEL

ONLY PLAYS "SUMMER-TIME," "IN THE MOOD," AND "TAKE THE A TRAIN."

SUMMERTIME... AND THE MUSIC IS TIRED...

The origins of this cartoon can be traced to my hearing "Ob-La-Di, Ob-La-Da" playing in a local coffee shop. The song stuck in my head, repeating over and over, becoming a sort of internal Ob-La-Di channel. It occurred to me that this experience was not a far cry from the micro-programming niches of satellite radio (such as the Elvis Channel).

So you know how dedicated I am to the accuracy of my cartoons, I actually watched a live concert video of Peter Frampton performing "Do You Feel Like We Do" on YouTube, even though I have always found the talkbox effect disturbing.

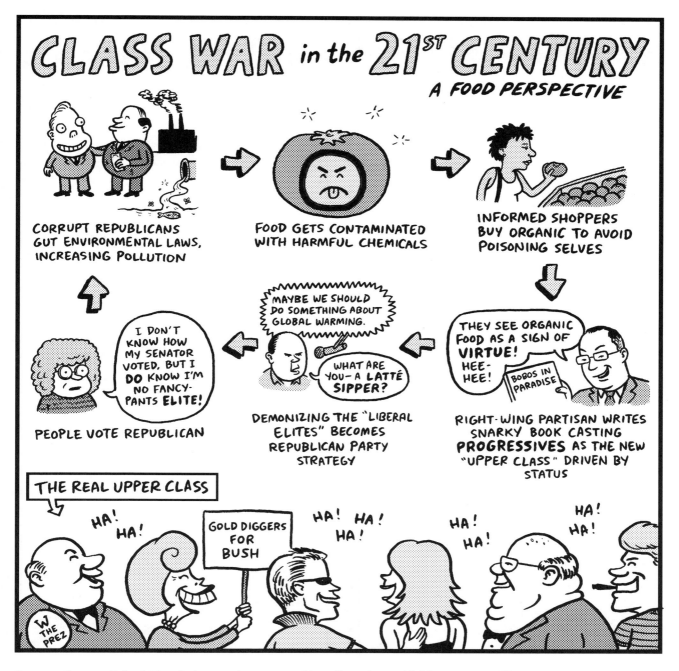

Conservative pundit David Brooks has made a career of branding educated lefties as snooty "liberal elites." His book *Bobos in Paradise* mocks the consumer habits of so-called bourgeois bohemians, describing signs at Fresh Fields advertising the number of organic items as a "barometer of virtue." Now, I sometimes make fun of new-agey marketing clichés in my cartoons (see the "Loona" bar, page 45), but being opposed to poisoning humanity does not make one an elitist.

Many progressives swallow the "liberal elite" narrative themselves, reproducing the right-wing frame. I call this participating in your own disempowerment.

STAND YOUR GROUND

15 STATES HAVE PASSED LAWS OVER THE LAST YEAR ALLOWING PEOPLE TO SHOOT FIRST EVEN IN NON-LIFE THREATENING SITUATIONS.

DON'T LOOK AT ME FUNNY.

LESS WELL KNOWN ARE THE LAW'S PREDECESSORS...

THE "CLAIM YOUR AIRSPACE" LAW— YOU MAY FORCIBLY INSERT A BALL GAG INTO THE MOUTH OF SOMEONE WITH HALITOSIS.

TAKE THAT, MAGGOT BREATH!

POONK!

THE "DEFEND YOUR FIELD OF VISION" LAW— PAINFUL WEDGIES MAY BE ADMINISTERED TO SOMEONE STANDING IN FRONT OF YOU WEARING A STUPID T-SHIRT.

YANK!

Moundy Mindy's BARE GRILL

SOON TO BE PASSED: THE "NAPALM FIRST" LAW

HOW WAS I TO KNOW HE WASN'T ABOUT TO NAPALM ME?

BETTER TO BE SAFE THAN SORRY!

PRIVATE PROPERTY

ACME HAIR BRUSHES

Merely living in America these days feels unsafe. Our health insurance system is broken, worker safety protections are being eroded, thousands of chemicals used in products have never been tested, people drive around in giant killer missiles blabbing on cell phones, the government wants to detain people as it pleases, there's hardly an economic safety net, and now your neighbor has more leeway than ever to shoot you if you're on his or her property. Contrast this to England, where people walk for fun, and public footpaths wind for miles through the countryside. Now *that's* freedom.

GOP PRESIDENTIAL HOPEFUL SENATOR GEORGE ALLEN SPARKED A CONTROVERSY RECENTLY BY ADDRESSING AN AMERICAN STUDENT OF INDIAN DESCENT WITH A RACIST SLANG TERM.

LET'S GIVE A WELCOME TO MACACA HERE! WELCOME TO AMERICA.

WE AT SLOWPOKE HELPFULLY OFFER SOME...

DAMAGE CONTROL
ADVICE for GEORGE ALLEN

OPTION 1: YOU WERE REALLY TRYING TO TOUT YOUR LOVE OF CHOCOLATEY CEREAL.

I'M CACA FOR COCOA PUFFS!

OPTION 2: ADMIT YOU USED A TERM FOR "MONKEY" BUT MEANT IT AS A COMPLIMENT!

MONKEYS CAN DO AMAZING THINGS WITH THEIR HANDS, YOU KNOW!

IF ALL ELSE FAILS, JUST EMBRACE YOUR INNER BIGOT!

PRESS

DAMN RIGHT I SAID "MACACA," BUCKWHEAT!

I must say, drawing this cartoon was satisfying. George Allen was my senator. He was the worst kind of regressive, pseudo-good ol' boy, southern-poser Republican with a well-documented history of racism, who should have had his Trent Lott moment years before the "macaca" incident. Yes, he actually had a noose hanging from a ficus tree in his law office!

The student he insulted, S.R. Sidarth, attended my alma mater, the University of Virginia. Since I still happened to live in Charlottesville, I gave Sidarth the original artwork of this cartoon. He was cool.

I own an iPod, but I'm partial to formats that take up three-dimensional space. When you're dealing with ephemeral creations like songs or (ahem) cartoons, it's nice to have them gathered together into a lasting volume. Half the joy of purchasing music is prying off the cellophane wrapper and unveiling the liner notes which, if you're lucky, contain candid photos of your favorite band getting drunk on tour. Sadly, children of the future may never know such pleasures.

"REFLECTING ABSENCE" AT GROUND ZERO

THE DEBRIS-FILLED LUNG MEMORIAL

I broke several of my own rules with this one—namely, the "show-don't-tell" rule, and the "try to be funny" rule—but this was a special occasion. In my opinion, the EPA's lie to New Yorkers that the air was safe to breathe after 9/11 when its own scientists suggested it was not was one of the worst crimes of the entire Bush era. The administration even deleted warnings for vulnerable segments of the population such as children, the elderly, or people with lung conditions.

This strip was a finalist in the Union of Concerned Scientists' "Science Idol" contest, which promoted cartoons about political interference in science.

SOCIAL NETWORKING SITES OF TOMORROW

SITES LIKE MYSPACE, FACEBOOK, AND FRIENDSTER ARE ALL THE RAGE. WHAT LIES AHEAD?

ANONYMOUSBOOK: A MEETING PLACE FOR THE INCOGNITO SET

Jane Doe

Sexual Preference: If I told you, I'd have to kill you.

Interests: Movies, maybe.

Jane Doe's Friends:
Mr. X   John Doe   Cipher   Deep Throat   Nobody

...OR BECOME A COMPLETE EXHIBITIONIST BY POSTING YOUR DNA ON GENESPACE.

COMMENT: I like the lay of your nucleotides!

genespace
"WHERE SEQUENCES MEET"

CHUCK

COMMENT:

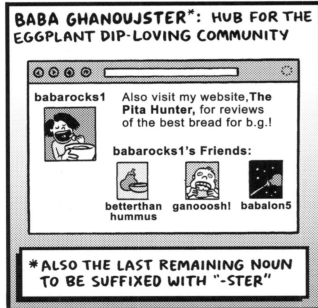

BABA GHANOUJSTER*: HUB FOR THE EGGPLANT DIP-LOVING COMMUNITY

babarocks1

Also visit my website, **The Pita Hunter,** for reviews of the best bread for b.g.!

babarocks1's Friends:
betterthan hummus   ganooosh!   babalon5

*ALSO THE LAST REMAINING NOUN TO BE SUFFIXED WITH "-STER"

BUDDHASPACE: THE ULTIMATE NETWORKING SITE — CONNECTS YOU TO THE ENTIRE UNIVERSE IN ONE CLICK!

BLANK SCREEN

OHM...

Social networking websites are getting a little out of control, don't you think? While researching the possible gag of Hamsterster, I found out there really is a hamsterster.com ("Your virtual hamster and gerbil community"). In fairness, the owner seems to have set it up as sort of a joke, though it is fully functional and contains over two thousand hamsters.

After making a big show of opposing torture, Sen. John McCain caved on a detainee treatment bill, the Military Commissions Act of 2006, which is what this cartoon is about. In short, it allowed torture, and did away with *habeas corpus* for whomever the president deems an "enemy combatant."

The idea for "terror grinders" came from an article I read about the civil war in Uganda, in which child-soldiers pulverized babies to death with a mortar and pestle. Not to make light of that situation or anything.

TWO-PARTY MONTE
...OR, "R2D II"

TRUE: ON BILL O'REILLY'S SHOW, REPUBLICAN PEDERAST MARK FOLEY WAS INCORRECTLY IDENTIFIED AS A DEMOCRAT **THREE TIMES.**

CROX NEWS
FORMER CONGRESSMAN MARK FOLEY (D-FL)

THIS GIVES KARL ROVE AN IDEA...

BUSH APPROVAL RATINGS

ÜBERMENSCH
HE'LL DO
PUTZ
SHOULD BE BURIED UNDER YUCCA MOUNTAIN

'02 '03 '04 '05 '06

I KNOW HOW TO WIN THE ELECTIONS... WE'LL CONVINCE THE PUBLIC DEMOCRATS HAVE BEEN RUNNING THE COUNTRY!

HEEHEEHEE... SQUEEEAL!

THE RE-EDUCATION PROCESS BEGINS...

THE DEMOCRATS HAVE FAILED TO CAPTURE BIN LADEN, STARTED A DISASTROUS WAR IN IRAQ THAT ONLY MADE TERRORISM WORSE, AND WANTED TO GIVE HOMELAND SECURITY FUNDING TO AN ARKANSAS **BEAN FEST!**

IT'S TIME TO PUT THE **REPUBLICANS** BACK IN CHARGE!

BUT-BUT- THEY HAVE BEEN!

HISTORICAL REVISIONIST!

CROX NEWS

AND SO... TIRED OF SCANDALS, RECKLESS SPENDING, AND ENDLESS WAR? IT'S TIME TO TAKE OUR COUNTRY BACK! VOTE MOE KRUPT, REPUBLICAN FOR SENATE!

HM. I COULD'VE SWORN—

TAKE THE COUNTRY BACK! YEAH!

Mark Foley was a gay Republican representative (with an anti-gay rights voting record, natch) who got caught sending salacious IM's to underage Congressional pages. Foley was erroneously identified as a Democrat three times on *The O'Reilly Factor*. I was reminded of the scene in *1984*, during Hate Week, when the government announces that the enemy is no longer Eurasia, but Eastasia. The rioting masses accept the change unquestioningly. I don't think O'Reilly fooled anyone, but if the Republicans *could* get away with convincing Americans that Democrats have been in charge the past several years, I think they might try.

SOME ON THE RIGHT CLAIM "TOLERANCE" IS TO BLAME FOR EVERYTHING FROM 9/11 TO THEIR OWN SEX SCANDALS. THEY MIGHT ALSO POINT TO THESE HISTORICAL EVENTS...

THE GREAT TOLERANCE WARS

VLAD THE OPEN-MINDED

I ACCEPT **YOU** MORE THAN YOU ACCEPT **ME!** **DIE!**

I RESPECTFULLY DISAGREE. **EAT MY SWORD!**

THE UNITARIAN CRUSADES

WE SHALL MARCH INTO THE LANDS OF THE DOGMATIC AND SPREAD FELLOWSHIP AND RESPECT FOR DIFFERING BELIEF SYSTEMS!

THE MULTICULTURAL PURGES OF 1914

IN OUR **EQUAL-OPPORTUNITY** GENOCIDE, WE'VE CHOSEN TO ELIMINATE MEMBERS OF ALL OF OUR GREAT NATION'S ETHNIC GROUPS!

THE POLYGLOT SUPREMACIST MOVEMENT

THIS HERE IS **MULTI-LINGUAL** COUNTRY!

IF YOU CAN'T SPEAK DUTCH, URDU, MANDARIN, ALEUT, AND ENGLISH, THEN **GET THE HELL OUT!**

Tony Perkins of the Family Reseach Council blamed Mark Foley's misbehavior on the "culture of tolerance." Quoth Perkins (no relation to the esteemed Slowpoke character): "When we hold up tolerance and diversity as the guideposts for public life, this is what you end up getting. You get congressmen chasing 16-year-olds down the halls of Congress. It's a shame." Got that? Be a bigot, or the pederasts win!

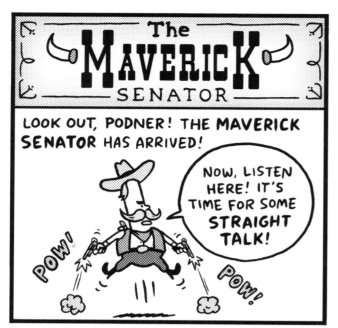

As you may have inferred, this one is about McCain. By talking a good game, he's managed to convince the punditry he's a "moderate" while maintaining a mostly-barbaric voting record. As of this writing, he gets an 82% lifetime rating from the American Conservative Union. Given how far right the envelope has been pushed in this country, that's hardly centrist. On the war and reproductive choice, he's downright extremist. And please—the man is hardly a font of "straight talk." He has flip-flopped on Bush's tax cuts, the religious radicalism of Jerry Falwell, and his own immigration bill. Indeed, the Mav panders with the best of 'em.

HEY, REPUBLICAN CANDIDATES! WANT TO TAKE YOUR ATTACK ADS TO THE **NEXT LEVEL**? TRY THE LATEST IN MUDSLINGING TECHNOLOGY: **SLANDERsoft™** **SMEARWARE 6.0!**

GO BEYOND THE TRADITIONAL "OPPONENT MORPHING INTO OSAMA" EFFECT WITH OUR LIBRARY OF 10,000 STOCK IMAGES!

RUNNING AGAINST A **BLACK MALE**? USE OUR STATE-OF-THE-ART CGI CAPABILITIES FOR THE ULTIMATE IN RACE-BAITING VISUALS!

JUST INSERT OPPONENT'S HEAD!

VOICEOVER: WHILE [YOUR NAME] WAS AT HOME READING STORIES TO HIS CHILDREN, [YOUR BLACK OPPONENT] WAS GETTING HIS FREAK ON IN NIGHT-CLUBS WITH **YOUR DAUGHTER!**

AND NOW, TWIST YOUR OPPONENT'S WORDS MORE EASILY THAN EVER WITH OUR INSTANT CONTEXT REGENERATOR!

I'D BE HONORED TO SERVE THE GREATEST NATION ON EARTH!

I'D BE HONORED TO SERVE THE GREATEST NATION ON EARTH!

ORDER NOW AND GET A FREE COPY OF PHOTO-OPS 9.1™ — NOW WITH MORE VIRTUAL BABIES!

The second panel of this cartoon draws on the infamously sleazy ad run against Vietnam vet and triple-amputee Sen. Max Cleland of Georgia, which coupled him with Osama. The third panel refers to an ad against Rep. Harold Ford of Tennessee, which used a white, bimboesque actress to subtly play into racial stereotypes. (Ford is black.)

After learning of my reference to Rob Halford, Mr. Slowpoke dug out his copy of *Judas Priest—Unleashed in the East* for inspiration while I drew the cartoon.

So... WE'VE SPENT **$339 BILLION** SO FAR ON A WAR JUSTIFIED BY TRUMPED-UP INTELLIGENCE THAT HAS KILLED 2,826 AMERICANS AND PROBABLY HUNDREDS OF THOUSANDS OF IRAQIS, MADE IRAQ RADIOACTIVE WITH DEPLETED URANIUM, AND CAUSED CIVIL WAR — ONLY TO MAKE TERRORISM **WORSE.** HECK, WE MAY AS WELL HAVE SPENT THAT MONEY ON...

SIX COPIES OF "MICHAEL BOLTON SINGS WHAM!" FOR EVERY PERSON ON EARTH. (NOTE: MAY INCITE JIHAD.)

SOLID GOLD CHENEY INSTALLED AS NEW MOON OF MARS

A STUPID DRUNKEN BET WITH PUTIN

A GIANT BUTT MADE OF 339 BILLION DOLLARS

A GIANT BUTT MADE OF 339 BILLION DOLLARS SET ON FIRE

The $339 billion figure, taken from the Cost of War counter on costofwar.com, was obsolete within days of publishing this cartoon. By the time this book is available, the counter should read close to $500 billion. Some future projections that include the cost of health care for injured veterans reach $2 trillion. That's a lot of Wham! albums.

I think the Democrats need to make a more forceful case for the jaw-dropping amount of taxpayer dollars being flushed down history's toilet. And also remind voters that the Republicans wanted to give antiterrorism funding to an Arkansas Bean Fest.

Reaching Out

THE PREZ GIVES HIS POST-ELECTION PRESS CONFERENCE.

WHEN I CAME TO WASHINGTON, I WANTED TO CHANGE THE TONE.

SO I WELCOME THIS OPPORTUNITY TO REACH OUT AND WORK WITH THE TERRORCRAT PARTY.

TO OUR ENEMIES, I SAY DO NOT BE JOYFUL THAT THE QAEDACRAT PARTY HAS WON. THAT'S JUST HOW DEMOCRACY WORKS SOMETIMES.

IT'S A BEAUTIFUL THING.

TO OUR TROOPS, I SAY DO NOT BE FILLED WITH DOUBT. I WILL WORK HAND IN HAND WITH THE SADDAMOCRATS TO MAKE SURE THEY DON'T SEND ANY IMPROVISED EXPLOSIVE DEVICES TO THE INSURGENTS TRYING TO KILL YOU.

THAT IS MY PROMISE.

IN CONCLUSION, I LOOK FORWARD TO DISCUSSING THE FUTURE OF THE COUNTRY WITH GREAT ISLAMOFASCICRAT LEADERS LIKE NANCY HEZBOLLOSI, HARRY RIYADH, AND BARACK OSAMA.

NOW, LET US BEGIN THIS NEW ERA OF POLITICAL HARMONY!

Bush's speech after the Republicans got a thumpin' in the 2006 elections was chock full of thinly-veiled insults: "The Democrat party." The awkward gender joke about Nancy Pelosi and drapes for her new office. And then this: "To our enemies, do not be joyful. Do not confuse the workings of our democracy with a lack of will... To the people of Iraq: Do not be fearful... To our brave men and women in uniform: Don't be doubtful. America will always support you." If anything, I imagine our enemies were disappointed that the party of total incompetence got the boot!

With studies predicting dramatic drops in snowfall and earlier melts, ski resort operators are panicked about global warming. I wonder what all those pooh-poohing fat cats with homes in Aspen will think when it's dry as a bone. To clarify, I'm not saying all skiers are Republican jerks. I like skiing plenty, even though it's too expensive.

The last panel was inspired by the $2 million, week-long birthday party in Sardinia for the wife of convicted Tyco CEO Dennis Kozlowski, which featured an ice sculpture of Michelangelo's David with vodka pouring out of his penis.

I had just finished reading, as a procrastinatory undertaking, Tom Lutz's *Doing Nothing: A History of Loafers, Loungers, Slackers, and Bums in America*. Some of our greatest Americans were slackers, you know. Benjamin Franklin was a lush who loved to take "air baths" in which he lay naked on his bed for an hour a day. Interestingly, many self-professed idlers were in fact workaholics, and vice-versa.

It occurred to me during one bout of procrastination that putting off work can sometimes be more laborious than the work itself. So why not commodify it?

APOLOGIES TO M. GROENING

This cartoon cites a study published in the *American Journal of Public Health* that showed that Philip Morris's anti-smoking ads urging parents to warn children against smoking actually intensified teenagers' desire to smoke. This of course comes as no surprise after the dorky campaign, "Tobacco Is Whacko If You're a Teen."

Some readers thought the rock star in the third panel was Keith Richards, but he's actually based on Johnny Thunders. By the way, I have seen Keith Richards with his shirt off, and it's not a pretty sight.

This strip finds Mr. and Mrs. P at the mall once again, in a reprise of the previous year's Christmas shopping cartoon. Little does Auntie Perkins know how much effort goes into finding her presents.

At some point, Hickory Farms changed the font of their logo from the campy one I tried to approximate in the first panel to a bland serif, but the original lettering—which I took in at Park City Mall throughout my youth—remains permanently etched in my brain.

SUSPICIOUS MINDS

GLOBAL WARMING DENIERS ARE QUICK TO CAST DOUBT ON THE MOTIVES OF ENVIRONMENTAL GROUPS.

THEY'RE JUST USING GLOBAL WARMING AS A **SCARE TACTIC** TO LINE THEIR POCKETS!

KOOK SCIENCE SPEWER MICHAEL CRICHTON

HERE'S HOW THEY MIGHT EXPLAIN OTHER CAUSES:

SOUP KITCHEN VOLUNTEERS ARE JUST IN IT FOR THE FREE SOUP!

MOTHERS AGAINST DRUNK DRIVING JUST WANT ACCESS TO PARTIES AT THE M.A.D.D. MANSION!

THESE PEACE CORPS PEOPLE ARE ONLY AFTER FREE MOSQUITO NETTING AND EXOTIC TOILETS!

NPR PLEDGERS DON'T REALLY LIKE LISTENING TO NPR. THEY JUST WANT THE **TOTE BAG!**

MOTHER TERESA WAS JUST LOOKING AFTER HER LEGACY, THAT **SELFISH BITCH!**

Michael Crichton's novel, *State of Fear*, suggested that environmental groups are just using global warming as a scare tactic to raise money. This meme, I have found, is astoundingly prevalent in right-wing media. Readers have emailed me parroting it. I only wish they would take that healthy skepticism and apply it to the groups *denying* global warming, which tend to be libertarian think tanks that oppose any efforts to protect the public from the excesses of industry. Nope, no political or financial motives there! Much more likely that global warming is all about Greenpeace getting better office furniture.

The Rise and Fall of a Gizmo

GIZMO APPEARS, PRICED FOR MILLIONAIRES AND HARDCORE TECHNOPHILES

EVENTUALLY THE PRICE DROPS, AVAILING GIZMO TO THE MASSES

GIZMO ATTAINS SACRED STATUS IN THE HOME

KNOCKOFFS PROLIFERATE

TWO YEARS LATER, GIZMO RETIRED TO STORAGE CLOSET

20 YEARS LATER, RETRO-ELECTRONIC DANCE OUTFIT NAMES SELF AFTER GIZMO

A MILLENIUM LATER, ALIENS FIND THE GIZMOS MAKE NICE HATS.

I've always thought it strange how the most amazing high-tech gadgets quickly become junk. My old laptop was a mean machine back in 1999, and an object of ridicule by the time I drew this cartoon in 2006. (I am attached to my old ten-pound portable, and still use it on occasion despite the wisecracks of those around me.) How swiftly—and yet almost imperceptibly, not unlike the human process of aging—our sexy technology turns into laughable kitsch. It's rather poignant when you think about it.

When Nancy Pelosi was sworn in as the first woman Speaker of the House, the general tone of the news media was a very normalizing, "Wow, isn't that great?" as if this proved what an egalitarian society we'd become. While I'm happy to see a sister ready to assume global domination when Bush and Cheney choke on their cream puffs, my overall reaction was that we should have been reading about this in nineteenth-century history books. Our technology makes us feel like a highly advanced culture, but when it comes to electing a female head honcho, we lag behind many other countries like Jamaica and Argentina.

Visit the
GEORGE W. BUSH PRESIDENTIAL LIBRARY
CONSTRUCTION COST: ONLY $500 MILLION— LESS THAN TWO DAYS OF WAR IN IRAQ!

Be greeted BY FRIENDLY, IVY LEAGUE–EDUCATED COWBOYS!

POLYURETHANE COWS

GEORGE W. BUSH PRESIDENTIAL LIBRARY / DUDE RANCH

DEMOCRAT ENTRANCE

ASTROTURF

UNDERGROUND TORTURE CHAMBER

HOW-**DEE!** COME ON IN!

HARVARD MBA

View RARE PHOTOS!

BILL MURRAY IN STRIPES

Condoleeza Rice tutors the president in foreign policy.

Pose WITH LIFE-SIZE REPLICAS OF THE PRESIDENT IN HIS YOUTH!

THE CHEERLEADER-IN-CHIEF!

'70s PLAYBOY

NATIONAL GUARD (THE AWOL YEARS)

See...

THE ACTUAL SHOW TURKEY HE PRESENTED THE TROOPS IN IRAQ FOR THANKSGIVING!

Kids! TRY TO TOP THE PRESIDENT'S DONKEY KONG SCORE IN THIS INTERACTIVE EXHIBIT!

HIGH SCORE 87913 POTUS 43

We're Sorry... THE IRAQ VICTORY ROOM ISN'T OPEN YET.

UNDER CONSTRUCTION INDEFINITELY

Housed at Southern Methodist University, the most expensive presidential library in history will supposedly come with a new neocon think tank called the (gag!) Institute for Democracy. Apparently purging blacks from voter rolls, fighting a vote recount in the closest presidential election in history, and operating in unprecedented secrecy are democratic ideals. Who knew? Interestingly, SMU's School of Theology opposes the Bush library, stating: "We count ourselves among those who would regret to see SMU enshrine attitudes and actions widely deemed as ethically egregious." Obviously a bunch of disgruntled Chomskyites, those theologians.

AMONG THE OTHER DUBIOUS HEALTH CARE PROPOSALS IN HIS STATE OF THE UNION SPEECH, THE PRESIDENT ONCE AGAIN FLOGGED **HEALTH SAVINGS ACCOUNTS**. SAVING YOUR OWN MONEY SEEMS TO BE THE REPUBLICANS' SOLUTION TO EVERYTHING. WHAT OTHER "PERSONAL ACCOUNTS" ARE NEXT?

LAID OFF? OPEN A **PERSONAL WELFARE ACCOUNT** AND EARN TAX-FREE CAPITAL GAINS ON YOUR **INVESTMENT PORTFOLIO!**

SLAYER

HOW MANY SHARES OF GOOGLE CAN I GET FOR THIS HUBCAP?

TO HELP WITH THE RISING COST OF EDUCATION, COLLEGE STUDENTS MAY INVEST THEIR TRUST FUNDS IN A TAX-FREE **PERSONAL PIZZA ACCOUNT.*** ALSO GOOD TOWARDS CALZONES, PASTA, AND GARLIC BREAD!

FOR EVERY POINT INTEREST RATES GO UP, I GET SIXTY PIZZAS! **SWEET!**

* NO TRUST FUND? NO PIZZA!

THE PERSONAL BAIL ACCOUNT WORRIED THAT CORPORATE CRIME COULD CATCH UP WITH YOU SOMEDAY? SET ASIDE SOME CASH FOR BAIL IN THIS TAX-FREE PLAN!

THE WORSE YOU'VE BEEN, THE MORE YOU'LL SAVE!

SHREDMAXX

THE TAX SHELTER FOR FAT CATS SAVINGS ACCOUNT OH, HELL. LET'S BE HONEST. THAT'S WHAT ALL OF THIS IS ABOUT ANYWAY. MINIMUM CONTRIBUTION: $20 MIL/ YEAR

FINALLY A **SIMPLE** WAY TO AVOID TAXES!

IT'S NICE TO SEE THE GOVERNMENT BECOMING MORE EFFICIENT!

Continuing with my ongoing tirade against "private savings accounts" as the answer to all social ills, I get a kick out of the idea that we can solve America's health care crisis with a tax shelter. As a self-employed person, I already pay for much of my health care through a personal account. It's called my checkbook. Really, it's like they're trying to sell you your own pants.

The "CWA" graffiti in the first panel alludes to a collective to which I belong called Cartoonists With Attitude.

Every so often, something happens that reminds you viscerally of the supremely unfair, amoral nature of the universe. For me, the death of Molly Ivins was one of those things. A genuinely funny woman with whom I agreed more consistently than perhaps any other pundit, Molly was often a source of inspiration to me. Her columns planted the seed for more than one Slowpoke cartoon. I found this one tricky to create, partly because I was upset, and partly because it's challenging to do an obituary cartoon without lapsing into the well-worn clichés of daily editorial cartoons (e.g., the deceased arriving at the pearly gates).

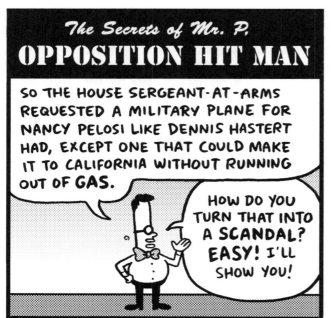

The mainstream media fell so hard for this right-wing booby trap, were you not paying close attention, you might think Pelosi had asked for a luxury jet to fly back to her home state. The House Sergeant-at-Arms simply requested a plane for Pelosi that could reach California (former Speaker Dennis Hastert had been granted a military plane to return to Illinois). Some Congressional Republicans pulled a PR stunt and promoted the most outlandish possibility: a fully-loaded 757. The story was all over cable news, and the *Washington Post* featured a photo of a 757 with their article. People are suckers for plausible narratives that confirm stereotypes, no matter how untrue they may be.

HEY, GOURMANDS! CHECK OUT THE LATEST GADGETS FOR...

THE 21ST CENTURY CHEF

THE V-CHIP (VEGGIE CHIP)-EQUIPPED GUILT-O-MATIC DINNER PLATE DETECTS WHEN YOUR KID HAS NOT EATEN HER GREENS AND ACTUALLY CAUSES FOOD TO BE WITHHELD FROM A STARVING CHILD IN AFRICA!

WIRELESS INTERNET SIGNAL

THE CELEBRIGRIDDLE GENTLY BROWNS THE FACES OF YOUR FAVORITE STARS INTO YOUR FLAPJACKS!

JAPANESE SNOW MONKEY RICE COOKER THE CUTEST APPLIANCE EVER! BOUNCES UP AND DOWN TO SHONEN KNIFE AND BJÖRK'S GREATEST HITS WHEN RICE IS READY!

RICE IN

THE SALAD UZI ADDS EXTRA FIREPOWER TO THE TRADITIONAL SALAD SHOOTER SO MEN FEEL COMFORTABLE USING IT.

INTO THE BOWL, DEAR!

FAP-FAP-FAP-FAP!

Mr. Slowpoke and I purchased a ridiculously cute Japanese rice cooker that plays "Twinkle, Twinkle, Little Star" when you set the timer, and a celebratory melody when the rice is ready. It looks like a giant stainless steel bug, and proudly advertises that it contains some special technology called—I am not making this up—"Fuzzy Logic." The only way it could be cuter is if it had fur. Enter the snow monkey.

I drew this while on a trip to L.A. It became much more pertinent several months later, when the Writers Guild of America went on strike. Seriously, why should actors get all the credit? Why should they get to live in Malibu palaces while the poor schlub writers tap away at their keyboards in dank hovels littered with Carl's Jr. wrappers and desiccated gummy bears stuck in the carpet? (I'm sure plenty of screenwriters live better than this, but please indulge me my rhetorical flourishes.) Writers create so much value in the entertainment industry, it is criminal what a small percentage of the profits they get.

Snickers ran a commercial during the Super Bowl showing two manly mechanics accidentally "kiss" while eating a Snickers Bar from opposite ends. They freak out and, in a bizarre display of machismo, start ripping out their chest hair. After gay rights groups complained, Snickers dropped the ad campaign. Then, a short while later, the cinematic abomination "Wild Hogs" was released. A buddy flick about four middle-aged guys on a motorcycle road trip, it featured oh-so-novel gags about people wrongly assuming the fellas were gay. Also around this time, Ann Coulter called John Edwards a "faggot." The yuks just don't stop!

"SHE LIKES HOW HE BLOGS, HER TEXTS TURN HIM ON," READS A NEW CALVIN KLEIN AD AIMED AT "TECHNOSEXUALS." NOW OTHERS HAVE PICKED UP ON THE TREND...

LOOKING TO GET YOUR GEEK ON WHILE YOU GET YOUR FREAK ON? THEN COME ON DOWN TO... **Drooly Julie's TECHNOSEXUAL Pleasure Palace**

We've Got:

STATUS MESSAGE SHIRTS THESE DIGITAL MARVELS PROJECT AVAILABILITY TO POTENTIAL SUITORS!

THE iPHONE *Eros*™ COMES WITH A ONE-TOUCH BOOTY CALL FEATURE THAT MAKES YOUR HONEY'S PHONE PLAY RIBALD RINGTONES!

BOOTY BUTTON — LET'S GET IT ON... ♫

PINK SATIN — LEOPARD PRINT — STUDDED LEATHER

L33T PORN FOR ULTRA-GEEKS

BLUETOOTH VIBRATORS LET YOU WIRELESSLY PROGRAM UP TO 18 DIFFERENT SETTINGS FROM YOUR COMPUTER!

...AND EMOTICONDOMS!

INTELLIBUZZER 5000
1. GENTLE HUM
2. RANDOM FLURRIES
3. SEISMIC BLAST

"LET'S GET GOOFY"

"PATRIOTIC SALUTE"

In its marketing campaign for the Gen-Y fragrance "in2u," Calvin Klein went so far as to trademark the term "technosexual." I immediately knew I had to do a cartoon about this exciting new demographic. To my delight, the term "emoticondoms" yielded no hits on Google. The Bluetooth vibrators are another story, as more than one reader pointed out to me. (I'm not sure what this says about my fan base.) This particular field of technology even has a name, which I hereby declare to be my favorite word of all time: *teledildonics*. It includes remote-controlled vibrators, virtual reality suits, and something called the Thrillhammer that you really don't want to know about.

A Poverty of News

IRAQ IS A BIG DEAL, NO DOUBT ABOUT IT. BUT WHAT IF OTHER ISSUES—LIKE POVERTY—GOT THE SAME KIND OF NEWS COVERAGE?

EMBEDDED REPORTERS

I'M HERE WITH KATE HAGGARD, SINGLE MOTHER OF THREE.

EVERY DAY HERE IS A MAJOR BATTLE!

ZING!

NIGHT-VISION CAMERA WORK
HERE WE SEE EXCLUSIVE FOOTAGE OF LARRY REEVES RISING AT 4 A.M. TO CLEAN THE TOILETS AT BOJANGLES'.

THERE'S NOT MUCH LIGHT SINCE HIS POWER WAS CUT OFF, BUT WE CAN STILL WATCH HIM IN ACTION THANKS TO THE MIRACLE OF TECHNOLOGY!

INTERVIEWS WITH EXPERT OFFICIALS

AND NOW WE TURN TO FELICIA HERNANDEZ, WHO HAS BEEN POOR FOR 38 YEARS! FELICIA, WHAT'S THE SITUATION ON THE GROUND?

IT'S COLD AND HARD, ROB.

STORIES ABOUT HEROISM

PROFILES IN COURAGE

DAVE PUTNAM WORKED THREE JOBS UNTIL HE LOST HIS LEG IN A SAUSAGE PLANT. HE HAS NO HEALTH INSURANCE, AND CAN'T DECLARE BANKRUPTCY BECAUSE OF THE 2005 BANKRUPTCY BILL. YET HE STILL KEEPS ON EXISTING!

YOU'RE AN INSPIRATION TO US ALL!

SHUT UP.

As I mention in the strip, I'm not saying Iraq isn't important. It's pretty damn egregious if I say so myself. But as John Edwards has said, "It's time for us to be patriotic about something besides war." The news media tend to elevate the importance of military matters above domestic concerns (that is, whenever they aren't talking about coked-up celebrity bimbos). Issues that affect millions of Americans, like the bankruptcy bill, receive comparatively scant coverage.

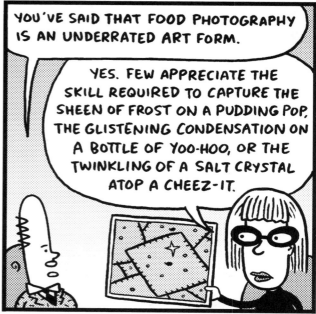

I've spent a lot of time staring at cereal boxes admiring the lush product photography while munching on my morning bowl. They tend to feature breathtaking shots of giant strawberries plunging into mounds of benuggeted flakes, causing the milk to splash upwards in playful arcs of wholesome goodness. Who takes these pictures, anyway? Are there special awards for cereal photography? It's a skill, to be sure.

For a while, this cartoon was mentioned in the Wikipedia entry for Cheez-its, but then some prig deleted the "Cultural References" section.

I am surprised how few people talk about events like the Virginia Tech shootings as media spectacles. As Cho Seung-Hui's "media kit" made plain as day, these massacres are not just about killing people; they are about fame. By releasing his home video and other materials, NBC played right into his hands. NBC actually *branded* the video with their logo, making the text of my third panel even more apropos than I'd thought.

This cartoon has the grim honor of being included in an online archive at Virginia Tech of events surrounding that day.

FACTOID FUN

THIS WEEK: SPOTLIGHT ON JOHN EDWARDS' HAIR!

BROUGHT TO YOU BY...

SMARTBOMBS™

BREAKFAST CEREAL

SMART BOMBS

"Treat your cranium to depleted uranium!"

FROM THE "WHAT'S MORE WASTEFUL?" DEPT... THE NUMBER OF JOHN EDWARDS' HAIRCUTS IT TAKES TO EQUAL ONE IRAQ WAR IS 1.05 BILLION AND COUNTING. THAT'S ONE HAIRCUT A WEEK FOR THE NEXT 20 MILLION YEARS!

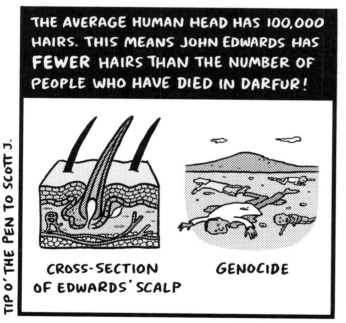

THE AVERAGE HUMAN HEAD HAS 100,000 HAIRS. THIS MEANS JOHN EDWARDS HAS FEWER HAIRS THAN THE NUMBER OF PEOPLE WHO HAVE DIED IN DARFUR!

CROSS-SECTION OF EDWARDS' SCALP

GENOCIDE

TIP O' THE PEN TO SCOTT J.

IF JOHN EDWARDS' HAIR HAD BEEN PRESIDENT FOR THE PAST FEW YEARS, THE COUNTRY WOULD BE IN *BETTER SHAPE THAN IT IS NOW!*

SHOULD WE ESCALATE IN IRAQ, SIR?

I'LL TAKE YOUR SILENCE AS A "NO."

YOU KNOW, WE COULD FIRE U.S. ATTORNEYS WHO DON'T ABUSE THEIR POWER.

ER— OR NOT.

I didn't want to give the Edwards haircut story any more legs, but once a stupid "scandal" like this has made its way through the cable news cycle, late night comedy shows, and a presidential candidates' debate, there's not much damage an altweekly cartoonist can do by continuing to talk about it. I issued an open invitation to the Edwards campaign: the next time someone brings up the silly haircuts, invoke my factoid that he could get one of those expensive do's every week for the next *twenty million years* and still not equal the cost of the Iraq War. As far as I know, my advice was not taken.

Let me just say I mock because I love. Okay, I'm not sure that I love the bongo-beaters who show up at political rallies—those events are *not* the place to let your freak flag fly. Someone did, sadly, set himself on fire to protest the Iraq War. He was not in his living room, but near a freeway exit in Chicago. As we can see, this strategy did not result in the desired policy change.

I considered including "political cartooning" among the activities listed here but, well, I like to think it has the potential to do *some* good.

Mr. Slowpoke read me something about an old Victorian medical practice of spinning people in centrifuges to balance out their bodily humors, which struck me as decidedly hilarious. I confess to taking a little artistic license here, placing the centrifuge back in the Middle Ages. The mingling of physical science and the supernatural that took place then would make today's Republicans feel right at home.

IT'S THAT TIME OF YEAR AGAIN! HERE'S A GLIMPSE AT THE UPCOMING

SUMMER BLOCKBUSTERS

WILL FERRELL IN
101 CHEESY GUYS

YOU'VE SEEN HIM AS A '70S ANCHORMAN, A NASCAR DRIVER, AND AN OLYMPIC ICE SKATER. NOW SEE HIM AS **101 KITSCHY CHARACTERS** IN ONE MOVIE — FROM MICHAEL JACKSON IMPERSONATOR TO SOFT-PORN LOTHARIO TO BRYLCREEM SALESMAN!

OVER 70 IRONIC MUSTACHES GUARANTEED!

MORE GODDAMNED PIRATES

IN THIS SEQUEL TO "PIRATES," "PIRATES TOO," AND "MILKING THE PIRATE THING AS LONG AS WE CAN," JOHNNY DEPP ONCE AGAIN MAKES PIRATES SEEM CUTE AND LOVABLE.

> AHOY, SUCKERS!

WARNING: PIRACY OF THIS FEATURE IS PUNISHABLE BY DEATH.

SCAT ATTACK

FILLING A LONGSTANDING VOID IN HOLLY-WOOD MOVIES, COLONIC HUMOR MAKES A BIG SPLASH IN THIS HILARIOUS ROMP!

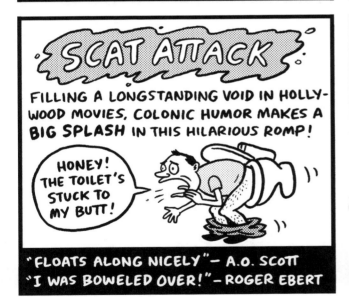

> HONEY! THE TOILET'S STUCK TO MY BUTT!

"FLOATS ALONG NICELY" – A.O. SCOTT
"I WAS BOWELED OVER!" – ROGER EBERT

CGI *Casablanca*
STARRING SHREK AS RICK!

A DIGITALLY-ANIMATED VERSION OF THE CLASSIC FILM UPDATED FOR GENERATION NOW!

> HERE'S LOOKIN' AT YOU, KID.

> WE'LL ALWAYS HAVE PIXELS.

Continuing with my campaign against ironic mustaches, if I see one more movie featuring a "wacky" male lead with goofy facial hair, I'm gonna plotz. These cloying attempts to appeal to my generation's sense of humor make me want to be stone-cold serious. And don't get me started on those pirate movies. I used to think Johnny Depp was kind of hot before he started dressing like some cheap baubled clown. I've also had enough of Shrek, who peered at me from a cereal box in the grocery store not long before I drew this. Can we at least get some *new* hollow characters to follow us everywhere we go?

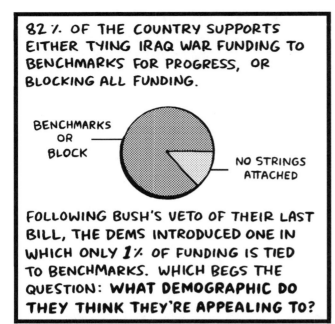

82% OF THE COUNTRY SUPPORTS EITHER TYING IRAQ WAR FUNDING TO BENCHMARKS FOR PROGRESS, OR BLOCKING ALL FUNDING.

BENCHMARKS OR BLOCK

NO STRINGS ATTACHED

FOLLOWING BUSH'S VETO OF THEIR LAST BILL, THE DEMS INTRODUCED ONE IN WHICH ONLY *1%* OF FUNDING IS TIED TO BENCHMARKS. WHICH BEGS THE QUESTION: **WHAT DEMOGRAPHIC DO THEY THINK THEY'RE APPEALING TO?**

POSTMODERN PHILOSOPHERS?

"PROGRESS" IS THE ILLUSION OF LINEARITY IN A CHAOTIC UNIVERSE. ALL IS BUT LATERAL DRIFT IN THE SWIRLING SEAS OF MEANING.

BRAVO THAT THE DEMS RECOGNIZE THIS FOLLY!

THE ELUSIVE PRO-ENVIRONMENT, PRO-CIVIL RIGHTS, ENDLESS WAR DEMOGRAPHIC?

THERE MAY BE JUST ONE OF US, BUT WE VOTE!

END RACISM

RENEWABLE ENERGY NOW

KILL'EM ALL

... OR THEY'RE TRYING TO APPEAL TO ALL AMERICANS, BUT USING POLLING DATA FROM 1962?

ACCORDING TO THIS, **NO ONE** SUPPORTS WITHDRAWAL FROM IRAQ!

After winning majorities in the House and Senate largely because of public opposition to the Iraq War, the Dems' cave on the funding bill was perplexing and infuriating to many. More than anything, Americans want leaders with convictions. For better or worse, it tends to matter less what those convictions are than their strength. By granting Bush a blank check to continue the gorefest, the Dems looked very weak. My own senator, Jim Webb, who had a son serving in Iraq, specifically cited the very pro-war Joe Lieberman in an explanation of his vote: "From the outset, we are a minority of 49, given Senator Lieberman's position on the war. This reality dictates our conduct."

That so many people get their knickers in a bunch about other people's purported "laziness" while being grossly misinformed themselves has always struck me as a tremendous double-standard. What I tried to do here was turn their language on welfare back on them. I imagine some might perceive this cartoon as "elitist" but in fact, they would be perceiving the elitism of their very own rhetoric about the poor. Personally, I prefer the thought of my taxes going to some poverty-stricken place in rural America (where a majority of welfare dollars are spent) than to crooked contractors in Baghdad. But that's just me.

DOES IT SEEM LIKE YOUR CREDIT CARD COMPANY CONSTANTLY SENDS YOU NEW CONDITIONS AND FEES?

SINCE DEREGULATION OF THE INDUSTRY BEGAN IN 1980, PROFITS FROM FEES HAVE SKYROCKETED. HERE ARE SOME MORE FEES WE CAN EXPECT IN THE FUTURE.

Due to your history of paying off your entire balance every month, we are instituting an "on-time" fee of $39. The late fee is now $39.50

TRADEMARK INSCRIPTION FEE — FEE FOR USE OF COMPANY'S NAME WHILE WRITING THEM A CHECK

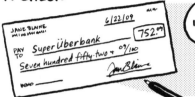

IT'S **OUR** INTELLECTUAL PROPERTY!

THE NON-PSYCHIC BILLING FEE — FOR HAVING BILLS SENT BY EMAIL RATHER THAN TELEPATHICALLY

CURRENT ACCOUNT BALANCE $1,182.39

UNCONVENTIONAL USAGE FEE — FOR USING CARD TO JIMMY OPEN LOCKED DOORS

THE CORRUPT CONGRESS FEE — IN HONOR OF THOSE WHO PASSED THE BANKRUPTCY BILL AND OTHER INDUSTRY-FRIENDLY LAWS

THE BORROWING MONEY WHILE POOR FEE — JUST IN CASE OTHER FEES, 30% INTEREST RATES, AND PREDATORY MARKETING AREN'T ENOUGH TO PUSH YOU OVER THE EDGE

"You're pre-approved to be our debt slave!"

JUST DOING THE WORK OF THE PEOPLE!

GIVE ME MY MONEY NOW.

THE COMPLAINING ABOUT FEES FEE — TINY VOICE RECOGNITION MICROCHIP IN YOUR CARD DETECTS KVETCHING, ALERTS CENTRAL COMPUTER

THIS FEE IS BULLS*!T!

ACCOUNT # 13978420-1246703 IS RESISTING.

When Mr. Slowpoke and I got our credit card bill after a trip to Toronto, we were shocked to find international transaction fees of 3% for every single purchase we made. This had not been the case when we'd used credit cards abroad in the past. According to *Consumer Reports*, the international fees started taking off around 2005, much to the consternation of the Consumers Union. On top of the fees, the exchange rate we got was lousy. Suffice it to say, the excesses of the credit card industry illustrate why we need consumer protections.

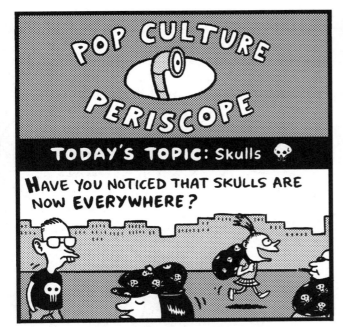

POP CULTURE PERISCOPE

TODAY'S TOPIC: Skulls 💀

HAVE YOU NOTICED THAT SKULLS ARE NOW **EVERYWHERE**?

USED TO BE, THEY WERE RESERVED FOR THE DEATH-RELATED...

FIG. A
TOXIC WASTE

FIG. B
METALHEAD

HYPOCRISY

BUT NOW THEY'VE GONE COMPLETELY **MAINSTREAM!**

AVAILABLE AT DEPARTMENT STORES!

Sears SALE!

WORN BY PSEUDO-PUNK POP STARS

SWEET-N-SASSY HEART AND CROSSBONES COMBO!

AVRIL LAVIGNE

BE ON THE LOOKOUT FOR **THIS**:

Baby's First Death's Head

AW, WE SHOULD SEND A PRINT TO GRANDMA!

While in Toronto, I noticed a number of people on the streets sporting skulls on their shirts, Chuck Taylors, etc. The department stores were all selling various skull-patterned items. And it's not just Toronto; they're everywhere. Mr. Slowpoke, who is something of a death metal connoisseur, is mildly outraged at this crass appropriation of cranial imagery by the masses.

The "Skull-a-Day" blog, presenting a skull-shaped art project every day for a year, featured a sewn "Baby's First Death's Head" toy apparently inspired by this cartoon.

SLOUCHING TOWARDS HYPOCRISY

AFTER A CAREER SPENT OPPOSING LAWSUITS FILED BY VICTIMS OF DISCRIMINATION AND INJURY, ROBERT BORK HAS FILED A $1 MILLION SUIT AGAINST THE YALE CLUB, WHERE HE TRIPPED CLIMBING ONTO A STAGE.

DON'T MESS WITH BORK!

HOW MIGHT HE POSSIBLY BE RATIONALIZING THIS?

HE'S BEEN POSSESSED BY HIS EVIL-TWIN LITIGIOUS POLTERGEIST

THE CIVIL COURTS ARE LIKE BARBARY PIRATE— ZOINKS!

I WANT PUNITIVE DAMAGES!

FULFILLING TEENAGE FANTASY OF VIOLATING TORT REFORM JUST ONCE

I WANNA BE BAD!

YOUNG BORKLET

SOMEDAY I'LL SUE SOMEONE.

RELYING ON THE "ONLY OLD, RICH, WHITE CONSERVATIVE WINDBAGS GET TO HAVE THEIR DAY IN COURT" EXCEPTION

SEE? IT'S RIGHT HERE!

THE FEDERALIST SOCIETY PLATFORM

We believe civil lawsuits impose undue costs on businesses, and therefore should be severely limited, except when the plaintiff is an old, rich, white conservative windbag.

When I found out Robert Bork was suing the Yale Club for injuries he sustained while climbing a stage, I knew I had a cartoon on my hands—partly because the hypocrisy was so juicy, and partly because it's so much fun to say "Bork." I was tempted to work in even more Borks, but restrained myself in the end. I'm not claiming Bork's suit is necessarily frivolous. The hypocrisy comes from his lack of sympathy for so many others who just wanted their day in court.

If I may be petty for a moment, Bork is not much of a looker. I was thinking, "Damn! It's like my cartoon got hit with the ugly stick!" But you gotta do what you gotta do.

This cartoon refers to missing girl *du jour* Madeline McCann, the latest in a string of attractive children whose disappearances are covered ad nauseum by cable news.

Hundreds of thousands of children are starving to death in the Congo because their mothers can't go into the fields without getting raped by soldiers. Meanwhile, celebrities are donating millions to find this missing British kid. If that isn't a sign of social sickness, I don't know what is.

This is the cartoon with the Ringo joke that Ruben Bolling mentioned in his introduction. I worked on it in between rounds of cocktails and banquet chicken at the Association of American Editorial Cartoonists' 50th annual convention in Washington, DC. I missed a luncheon featuring the cuddly Mark Shields because of it. How I suffer for my art!

The Kinks' "Picture Book" is one of my favorite songs of all time, and my memories of it were indeed mangled when I heard it accompanying a TV commercial for HP digital photography products.

Cults of America

THIS WEEK: THE MARKET LIBERATION ARMY

THE M.L.A. IS LED BY THE CHARISMATIC **CHARLES MANSION**, WHO CLAIMS TO CHANNEL THE LATE ECONOMIST MILTON FRIEDMAN.

FREE YOUR TRADE AND YOUR SOUL WILL FOLLOW!

MEMBERS LIVE IN A COMPOUND CALLED **DOW-JONESTOWN**, WHERE THEY ARE INDOCTRINATED WITH MARKET FUNDAMENTALISM.

HOW DO WE KNOW WHAT TO DO, O CHOSEN ONE?

TALK TO THE HAND... THE **INVISIBLE HAND!**

LET IT LIFT YOUR SPIRIT AND GUIDE YOU IN THE WAYS OF THE HOLY PROFITS.

THEY DEVELOP PARANOIA ABOUT THOSE ON THE OUTSIDE.

THE EVIL MINIONS OF THE **ANTI-HAND** ARE EVERYWHERE. WE MUST FIGHT THEIR **PUBLIC SCHOOLS** AND **POST OFFICES!**

THESE RAIMENTS MADE FROM **WALL STREET JOURNAL EDITORIAL PAGES** WILL PROTECT US FROM THEIR **SOCIALISM RAYS!**

Reagan Lives

Tyranny of the Poor

ANY SKEPTICISM IS QUICKLY QUASHED.

I'VE BEEN THINKING BAD THOUGHTS, O CHOSEN ONE... LIKE MAYBE WE SHOULD DO SOMETHING ABOUT GLOBAL WARM—

HUSH! THE MARKET WORKS IN MYSTERIOUS WAYS. BUT IT WILL **ALWAYS LOVE YOU.**

Though some in our binary-thinking culture may interpret this as an argument against all of capitalism, it's not. I am trying to show how overzealous worship of the "magic of the market" becomes a religious belief system, one that is about as tethered to reality as the teachings of various cults. We don't think of the disciples of Milton Friedman as cult members; after all, they look perfectly normal in their suits, and tend to keep their hair under control. (No offense to the well-groomed cult members out there.) But when a blind ideology trumps empiricism, fills people with purpose and wonder, and becomes the unassailable answer to anything, you're dealing with a form of faith.

FOX, CBS, and local affiliates of NBC and ABC refused to run a harmless commercial for Trojan condoms. The ad showed condom-eschewing pigs prowling around a bar looking for ladies. One of the pigs purchases a Trojan and becomes a studly dude. The tagline? "Evolve."

I'm more offended by the faux prudishness of these lite smut-peddling networks than I am by any condom ad. It's the 21st century, and we still can't talk about jimmy hats? Not even via computer-animated pigs? What the hell is wrong with us?

As expected, I heard from a couple angry readers who thought I was defending Michael Vick or downplaying the heinousness of his cruelty to animals. Let me just say that I am the owner of a massively cute dog, and was bothered by what Vick and his cohorts did as much as anyone. In the cartoon I'm trying to point out the disconnect between Americans' reaction to Vick, and their reaction (or lack thereof) to other kinds of cruelty towards humans. It's easier for us to blame humans for their circumstances, even if they have little control over them.

"LILLY LEDBETTER SUFFERED NEARLY TWO DECADES OF PAY DISCRIMINATION AT GOODYEAR. IN A 5-4 RULING, THE SUPREME COURT DENIED HER CLAIM BECAUSE SHE DIDN'T FILE WITHIN 180 DAYS OF THE INITIAL DISCRIMINATION, WHICH OCCURRED BEFORE SHE KNEW WHAT WAS GOING ON."

NOW GOODYEAR HAS BILLED HER $3,165 FOR COURT-RELATED EXPENSES!

WHAT'S NEXT FROM GOODYEAR?

The ALITO

ROLL OVER FAMOUS WOMEN'S RIGHTS SUPPORTERS!

"LET THEM EAT RUBBER!"

...AND BE ON THE LOOKOUT FOR THE NEW BLIMP!

Lilly Ledbetter acted as soon as she found out from an anonymous source that her male co-workers were being paid significantly more than she was. But the newly-radicalized Supreme Court, including Samuel "no ladies at Princeton" Alito, ruled that the statute of limitations runs out 180 days after the first discriminatory paycheck—long before most people discover they are being paid less than their peers. Democrats in Congress have introduced the Ledbetter Fair Pay Act clarifying that the 180-day period starts anew after each discriminatory paycheck. The fact that Goodyear sent Ledbetter a $3,000 bill after all of this assures that I will be driving on Michelins for the rest of my life.

When I was growing up, we didn't have "tweens." Kids eleven or twelve years old were called kids, or maybe sometimes preteens. How anyone can use the term "tweens" with a straight face is a mystery to me. I guess marketing people don't have these hangups. According to sociologist Juliet Schor in *Born to Buy*, "Researchers have chopped up the 52 million plus children in the age-twelve-and-under demographic into discrete age, gender, ethnic, and product segments, each with tailored messages."

I had been listening to a lot of Ween around the time that I drew this, which led to the reference at the end.

This one was conceived while on a trip to Ireland and written at some 35,000 feet over the Atlantic. A couple days into my vacation I found myself totally exhausted, wishing someone would just cart me around Dublin. Now, as a frequent jogger, I like to think I'm in halfway decent shape. I could only imagine what touring Europe must be like for non-perambulatory Americans. Thankfully for them, alternatives exist that aren't a far stretch from my cartoon. One tour company in Dublin drives people around the city in buses shaped like Viking ships. Some of the people in the ships wear Viking helmets, cheering loudly as they wend their way through the streets.

APPETITE FOR DESTRUCTION

THE WHITE HOUSE IS ISSUING A NEW RULE THAT WILL ALLOW MORE MOUNTAIN-TOP REMOVAL MINING.

MOUNTAINTOP BLOWN OFF, RAINING SULFURIC DUST

COAL EXTRACTED, WASTE DUMPED INTO STREAMS

COAL BURNED IN PLANT, CONTRIBUTING TO GLOBAL WARMING

MERCURY FALLOUT ENTERS BLOODSTREAM

THE WHOLE PROCESS DESTROYS MOUNTAIN RANGES, FORESTS, WATERWAYS, THE AIR, TOWNS, SEAFOOD, BABIES' BRAINS, AND ULTIMATELY THE PLANET. BUT WHY STOP THERE? WHY NOT TRY...

EARTH REMOVAL MINING

WITH OUR NEW, STATE-OF-THE-ART EXPLOSIVES, WE CAN TAKE OUT A HEMISPHERE IN LESS THAN A WEEK!

YES, THIS EFFICIENT NEW TECHNIQUE BLOWS AWAY **EVERYTHING** BUT THAT SWEET BITUMINOUS!

DEATH STAR 9000™

THAT WAS PORTUGAL.

OPERATI SUCCESS

IN THE END, WHAT'S LEFT WILL POWER THE ESCAPE ROCKET FOR THE EXECUTIVE BRANCH!

SEE YA! WOULDN'T WANNA BE YA!

One of the worst Bush administration acts you haven't heard about is their giving the green light to mountaintop removal mining. In addition to the details mentioned in the cartoon, the blasts release corrosive compounds into the air which are harmful to both people and structures. Processing coal literally produces mammoth toxic sludge ponds which have been known to spill into waterways. Vast parts of Appalachia are being destroyed, all for a filthy, antiquated source of energy we need *less* of if we hope to combat global warming. Future historians (assuming the human race survives) will look back on this practice as a testament to our awesome stupidity.

Senator Larry Craig, a staunchly anti-gay Republican from Idaho, was caught signaling an interest in sex during a sting in an airport men's room. According to David Brock's *Blinded By The Right*, Washington contains a sizable underground of closeted gay Repubs.

While discussing the Craig incident, conservative pundit Tucker Carlson chuckled on-air about hitting the head of a gay man who "bothered him" against a bathroom stall as a high school student. After receiving widespread criticism for his remark, he issued an explanation that struck a different tone, saying he had been assaulted.

MORE Accidental Hipsters

MANNY SPRECHER, 53

FAUCET SALESMAN

HAS WORN AVIATOR SHADES AND A MEMBERS ONLY JACKET FOR SO LONG THAT THEY EVENTUALLY BECAME COOL AGAIN

RANDY PUSHKIN, 64

AMBASSADOR TO TUNISIA

WEARS PUMA VISOR RAKISHLY SIDEWAYS – BUT ONLY FOR THE SUN PROTECTION

This week: Cat booties

OH MY GOD! CAN I GET YOUR PICTURE FOR KNITPUNKER MAGAZINE?

THE LAKE WINNIPESAUKEE KNITTING SOCIETY

STRANGELY UNAWARE OF THEIR PLACE IN THE CUTTING-EDGE, DIY CRAFT MOVEMENT

DO NOT PHOTOGRAPH THE HIPSTER

BOG HIPSTER 1,862 YEARS OLD

MUSEUM ATTRACTION

WITH TRIBAL-STYLE EAR PIERCINGS, TATTOOS, AND AN ARTFULLY UNKEMPT 'DO, THIS MAY WELL BE THE FIRST ACCIDENTAL HIPSTER!

A reprise of a popular cartoon I'd done several years earlier. When I was in Dublin I saw some mummified bog people at the National Museum, which provided inspiration for the bog hipster. Apparently the chemical composition of peat bogs in northern Europe preserves bodies very well. Bog people have been found with tattoos and plenty of hair; I threw in the plug-style earring myself, which may or may not be historically accurate.

Are You PETRAEUSLY CORRECT?

THE SENATE RECENTLY PASSED A RESOLUTION CONDEMNING AN ADVERTISEMENT THAT DARED TO CRITICIZE GENERAL PETRAEUS.

CONFUSED ABOUT WHAT YOU CAN AND CAN'T SAY ABOUT MEMBERS OF THE MILITARY? I'M PROFESSOR PERKINS, AND I'M HERE TO HELP!

DO QUESTION THE PATRIOTISM OF A TRIPLE-AMPUTEE VIETNAM VET, AS THE GOP DID IN ATTACK ADS AGAINST SEN. MAX CLELAND.

MAX CLELAND CLAIMS HE HAS THE COURAGE TO LEAD...

BUT HE'S REALLY OSAMA'S BEST HO!

DON'T DARE POINT OUT THAT GEN. PETRAEUS HAS POPPY SEEDS STUCK IN HIS TEETH FROM HIS BREAKFAST BAGEL.

WE'RE MAKING PROGRESS IN ANBAR!

DO MOCK JOHN KERRY'S WOUNDS FROM VIETNAM BY PASSING OUT "PURPLE HEART BAND-AIDS" AT THE REPUBLICAN NATIONAL CONVENTION.

KERRY GOT A WIDDLE BOO-BOO!

SNORT!

DON'T DROP A NEWSPAPER FEATURING A PHOTO OF PETRAEUS ON THE FLOOR. IF YOU DO, **YOU MUST KISS IT!**

I AM SO SORRY!

* TWO OF WHOM ARE NOW DEAD

DO DISMISS THE SOLDIERS WHO WROTE AN OP-ED IN THE NEW YORK TIMES THAT CONTRADICTED PETRAEUS' CLAIMS.*

IT WAS A LIBERAL PLOT.

WHATEVER YOU DO, **DON'T** DRAW THE GENERAL AS BUSH'S LEG-HUMPING LAPDOG!

GEN. POODLUS

THIS IS A BIG NO-NO!

PFUT

DOWN, BOY!

CONGRESSIONAL TESTIMONY

Before General David Petraeus testified about the Iraq War, MoveOn.org ran an ad that read "General Petraeus or General Betray Us?" suggesting that he'd become a partisan spin man for the White House—which in fact, he had. The wingnuts predictably accused MoveOn of hating the military. Then the U.S. Senate decided to wade into the matter. In an astonishing swipe at the First Amendment, they declared Gen. Petraeus to be off-limits to criticism, with 25 craven Democrats voting for the resolution. The poodle was inspired by a mini-controversy that erupted over Daryl Cagle's cartoon of Petraeus as Bush's pet dog. I decided to make him fluffier and gassier.

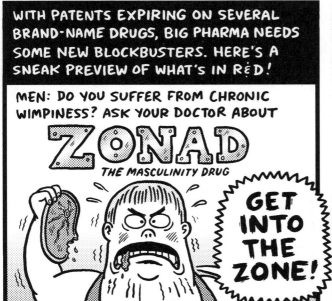

I've often thought that drug companies should team up with car makers and do a little cross-marketing, since both are prone to giving their products ridiculous names. Chevy Celebrex, anyone?

After doing this strip, I found out there is an obscure Irish film by the name of Zonad. The director has started reshooting the film, so perhaps "Zonad" will be a household word before long.

The GOP spends a lot of time trying to paint progressives as out-of-touch, ivory tower elites. But if anything, that distinction goes to the so-called "neocon intellectuals" like Norman Podhoretz, the inspiration for Dr. Plonk. In a 2007 *Wall Street Journal* editorial, Podhoretz said he prays "with all his heart" that we will bomb Iran, making the usual facile comparisons to World War II.

After making up the name "Plonk," I found out that it's an old geek term for blocking the posts of annoying users on usenet. "Plonking" someone involves adding them to your kill file. Perfect, huh?

The RECLAIM GAME

STAGE 1: THE INSULT

PENGUIN KISSERS!

HAW!

FIGHT GLOBAL WARMING

NO NEW COAL PLANTS

STAGE 2: THE IDEA

DAMMIT! I'M TIRED OF BEING CALLED A PENGUIN KISSER!

YEAH! HEY... LET'S TAKE THE TERM BACK!

STAGE 3: THE T-SHIRTS

Penguin Kisser

STAGE 4: IT'S EVERYWHERE!

HAVE YOU SMOOCHED A PENGUIN TODAY?

I ♥ FLIGHTLESS ANTARCTIC SEABIRDS

PENGUIN KISSER MONTHLY

SOLAR PANELS MADE E-Z

STAGE 5: THE NEXT ENCOUNTER

HEY, PENGUIN KISS— MY GOD!

MELTING OUR ICE ISN'T NICE

SAVE OPUS

NOW EVEN **THEY** THINK THEIR CAUSE IS ABOUT PENGUINS! THAT WORKED **BEAUTIFULLY!**

STAGE 6: THE CYCLE CONTINUES...

HEY, *COW HUMPERS!*

STOP ANTIBIOTICS IN MEAT

NO MORE BIONIC BOVINE

APOLOGIES TO DAN P. AND BERKELEY B.

There have been exceptions, but most of the time the effort to reclaim a regressive epithet fails as a political strategy. Among the worst is "tree hugger." Not wanting climatic catastrophe has little to do with the quasi-spiritual groping of conifers, yet that is how those of us concerned about the environment have been stereotyped. I mean, I like trees as much as anyone, but the term "tree hugger" is dripping with connotations of hippie-dippy hysteria. Using it ironically to reclaim it from the anti-science crowd may make us chuckle, but it's still letting them define us on their terms.

I drew this shortly after Al Gore won the Nobel Peace Prize. The strip actually began with the headless cow. I'd been thinking that there needs to be a new kind of meat; beef is full of cholesterol, *E. coli*, and possibly prions that will turn your brain into a sponge. Fish can contain mercury and PCBs, and other pollutants if it comes from places like China where it is often farmed in fetid water. As for pork, well, I'm ethically conflicted about eating something smarter than my dog. Wouldn't it be nice if we could develop a new kind of meat that grew more like a vegetable? I would love to go running through fields of meatballs.

AXIS OF THE EVIL DEAD

TRUE: THE CIA HAS POSTED AN OFFICIAL "TERRORIST BUSTER" LOGO ON ITS WEBSITE.

REMARKABLY CRAPPY DESIGN!

PRESIDENT BUSH EXPLAINS:

AS PART OF THE AXIS OF THE EVIL DEAD...

IRAN MUST NOT OBTAIN ECTOPLASMIC GOO!

THE WHITE HOUSE TURNS TO OTHER OLD SCI-FI MOVIES TO HELP WITH ITS WAR EFFORT

BLAARR!

AN ARMY OF LINDA BLAIRS FROM "THE EXORCIST" WILL SCARE THE PANTS OFF INSURGENTS!

E.T. WILL BE ENLISTED TO THROW REESES PIECES AT GRATEFUL CHILDREN.

MAY WE SUGGEST THESE LOGOS AS WELL?

"BUDGET BUSTERS" FOR THE ENTIRE ADMINISTRATION

"CHILD-BUSTERS" FOR REPUBLICANS OPPOSED TO S-CHIP

INSURING KIDS? NOW THAT'S SCARY!

It's still unclear to me whether the terrorist buster logo is an example of CIA "humor" or a semi-serious undertaking. In any event, the original is an object lesson in Things Not to Do With Photoshop. Also, the terrorist is anatomically incorrect.

I'm not above making *Ghostbusters* references myself (see "Memebusters," page 88). But then, I'm a cartoonist, and the CIA is... well... the CIA. I guess it's nice to think that someone there has a sense of humor. Maybe the logo is intended as an ultra-ironic statement on War-on-Terror jingoism. In that case, it would be very sophisticated.

For so long, we Americans have reaped the benefits of cheaper foreign currencies; we've stuffed our homes with all sorts of imported appliances, and with a bit of saving, the middle class could afford to visit most countries. Now we find these luxuries eroding. While I doubt we'll be making fruit hats for Brazil anytime soon, Brazilian immigrants are reportedly leaving the U.S. in droves because of the booming economy there and the falling dollar. Soon travel to Europe could be another exclusive province of the rich. I like to think of it as the Bush Travel Tax: "No *dolce vita* in Florence for you, sucker! You're going to Disneyland!"

Sitting on Their Asses

WITH FEW EXCEPTIONS, CONGRESSIONAL DEMOCRATS HAVE FAILED HORRIBLY AGAINST THE BUSH ADMINISTRATION.

HERE ARE SOME WAYS THE DEMS COULD BE **MORE USEFUL** THAN THEY HAVE BEEN!

AS PAPERWEIGHTS FOR HILL STAFFERS

DEMOCRATIC SENATOR

NOW THE PETITIONS FROM HER CONSTITUENTS ASKING HER TO **DO SOMETHING** WON'T BLOW AWAY!

SITTING IN BED IN THEIR HOME STATES

...AND THE HOUSE APPROVED ANOTHER $50 BILLION TODAY FOR THE WAR IN IRAQ...

IT WOULD HAVE PASSED ANYWAY IF I'D BEEN THERE.

BY NOT FLYING TO DC, I'M REDUCING MY CARBON FOOTPRINT BIG-TIME!

STANDING UP TO BUSH IN GAME OF "FANTASY CONGRESS" SO AT LEAST VIRTUAL AMERICA ISN'T SCREWED

HA! I JUST FILIBUSTERED THAT PRO-TORTURE ATTORNEY GENERAL NOMINEE INTO OBLIVION!

TAKE THAT, SUCKERS!

This one followed the Democrats' rollover on Attorney General Michael Mukasey, who curiously didn't seem to have a problem with waterboarding. To their credit, the Dems have done a few things, like raise the minimum wage, force Bush to veto a children's health insurance plan, and introduce the Ledbetter Act against sex discrimination. But they remain consistently cowed by the threat of Republicans calling them "weak on terror." They're going to be smeared no matter what, so they may as well go on the offensive.

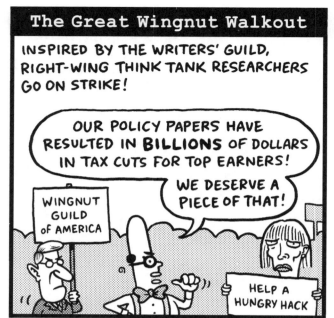

I drew this when the Writers Guild of America went on strike. I decided to have right-wing think tank workers go on strike instead. Both groups deal in fiction, so why not?

The third panel is a reference to a highly entertaining debate that happened on the *New York Times* op-ed pages. Paul Krugman had written about Ronald Reagan kicking off his 1980 campaign in Philadelphia, Mississippi, where three civil rights workers were murdered. David Brooks wrote a ridiculous piece making all kinds of excuses for Reagan, though even he couldn't rationalize away Reagan's defense of "states' rights" in regards to education, which was a clear appeal to segregationists.

Bob Allen, an anti-gay rights state senator and McCain campaign co-chair, approached a plainclothes cop in a restroom stall and offered to pay $20 to perform oral favors. He now claims he did this because *the cop was a burly black man and he was afraid he would get mugged.* Someone needs to tell these guys to shut up after getting caught.

The Klingon reference owed to the fact that I'd been watching episodes of the original *Star Trek* on DVD. You know what I really like about *Star Trek?* That they actually tried to titillate the ladies by showing Captain Kirk with his shirt off and/or torn in every other episode. It's so refreshing to have gratuitous skin aimed at us for a change!

After joining Facebook, I was amazed to find hundreds of virtual objects for sale that users could purchase to give to their Facebook friends. In addition to those mentioned in the cartoon, there are panties, puppies, cupcakes, hamburgers, polar bears...the list goes on and on. Sorry, but I would rather walk down the street singing "Zip-a-Dee-Doo-Dah" in a Smurf suit than be caught paying money for virtual cupcakes.

I hate the dark days leading up to the winter solstice. It's like a descent into hell. How Alaskans and Scandinavians deal with four hours or so of daylight is beyond me. I guess Finnish saunas, Swedish massages, and psychedelic northern lights go a long way.

Fortunately, my Australian readers seemed to have a sense of humor about the third panel. One was quick to point out that Mel Gibson was actually born in the United States, so they had no claim to "that nut-job."

First they were called "enduring bases." Then the name was changed to the even more *politically-correct* "contingency operating bases." But at this point, there can be little doubt that the super-size military bases being constructed in Iraq are not exactly disappearing anytime soon. The Bush administration flatly denies plans for "permanent military bases," which according to the Opposite Rule that applies to everything the Bushies say, means we are building permanent military bases.

The presidential primaries are not for the thinking person. All the nonstop chatter about the candidates' temperaments makes me wonder why I even bother to learn about things like, you know, issues. I drew this shortly after Hillary Clinton "got emotional" at a campaign stop just before the 2008 New Hampshire primary. Fox News trumpeted the headline "HILLARY'S BREAKDOWN," as though the senator from New York had just lost it Britney-style. (In fact, her voice had quavered slightly.) In this precarious time of war, global warming, a health care crisis, and economic woes, *this* is how we decide the leader of the most powerful nation on earth?

In 2005, then-Federal Reserve chief Alan Greenspan played down the possibility of a nationwide housing bubble, instead opting to use the pleasant, cappuccino-evoking term "froth." In late 2007, after the collapse of the subprime mortgage market, he exclaimed "no one expected it." But many economists had.

While the Dems improved the stimulus package slightly over the Republican version, the food stamp and unemployment benefits they agreed to nix would have kicked in faster than the tax rebates that passed. Chalk up another victory for ideology over efficiency.

CHRIS MATTHEWS, NAD DEFENDER

HERE'S HOW POLITICAL COMMENTATOR CHRIS MATTHEWS DESCRIBED HILLARY CLINTON'S ENDORSERS:

AREN'T YOU APPALLED AT THE WILLINGNESS OF THESE PEOPLE TO BECOME **CASTRATOS** IN THE **EUNUCH CHORUS**?

MATTHEWS WAS CLEARLY REFERRING TO A RECENT STUDY PUBLISHED IN THE NEW ENGLAND JOURNAL OF MEDICINE.

OUR MODELS INDICATE THAT, IF A **WOMAN** BECAME PRESIDENT, ALL THE NATION'S NADS WOULD SPONTANEOUSLY DETACH FROM THEIR OWNERS!

A.   B.

SOME SAY THAT THE 150 MILLION SETS OF COJONES WOULD BE CRYOGENICALLY FROZEN BY WICCANS AND HELD HOSTAGE TO HILLARY'S AGENDA.

I WILL RELEASE 10,000 FAMILY JEWELS FOR EACH OF MY HEALTH CARE PROPOSALS THAT IS ENACTED!

NOW **THAT'S** POLITICAL CAPITAL!

THOSE EAGER TO REDEEM THEIR MANHOOD COULD EARN BOLLOCK REDEMPTION POINTS BY SINGING IN A **EUNUCH CHOIR**.

♪ OUR BITS WERE TAKEN BY HIL-LARY AND NOW WE SOUND LIKE GED-DY LEE! ♪

HIT THOSE HIGH NOTES, CHRIS!

HRUMPH! SEEMS PLAUSIBLE TO ME!

In addition to the castration comment addressed in the cartoon, Chris Matthews has questioned how women can give emphatic speeches without sounding like "fingernails on a chalkboard"; he has called Hillary "witchy," a "she-devil," "anti-male," and compared her to Nurse Ratched. He has also spoken of Nancy Pelosi castrating Rep. Steny Hoyer. As I was writing this strip, Matthews actually issued an on-air apology for saying Hillary had only gotten as far as she had because her husband fooled around. But he mainly focused on that one statement, which was far from his worst, in my opinion.

FYI, most Wiccans are not scowling ball-busters in pointy hats.

A host of new services catering to the super-rich allow them to practically live in a separate universe from the rest of us mortals. Luxury airlines like EOS shuttle them around in supreme comfort (beds over six feet long!). For a pretty penny, "boutique" physicians offer the kind of personal, round-the-clock care people received from doctors of yore. When the most privileged and powerful members of society can escape the hassles and declines in service the rest of us must put up with, there's that much less impetus for change. Some might say, "They're paying for it. Get over it." While I understand that reasoning, it seems limited in scope, failing to question the larger system that created the neo-aristocracy in the first place.

Panel 1: DEMOCRATS ARE AT EACH OTHER'S THROATS OVER THE PRESIDENTIAL CANDIDATES.

Obama / Hillary

WAR-MONGERING TRIANGULATOR!

OVERHYPED HEALTH CARE DEMAGOGUE!

Panel 2: AS THE RACE DRAGS ON, THE DNC DECIDES TO UNITE THE PARTY WITH A MEDICAL MIRACLE.

LADIES AND GENTLEMEN, I PRESENT TO YOU... OBALLARY!

NOW THAT'S CHANGE!

Panel 3: OBALLARY'S ABILITY TO SIMULTANEOUSLY EAT WAFFLES WHILE GIVING STUMP SPEECHES IN SMALL-TOWN DINERS ALLOWS IT TO COVER TWICE AS MANY CAMPAIGN STOPS AS USUAL.

GMORF!

LEMME TELL YOU ABOUT HOPE.

Panel 4: THE OBALLARY CAMPAIGN QUICKLY WINS OVER THE PRIZED SIAMESE TWIN AND SCI-FI NERD VOTE.

FINALLY! SOMEBODY WHO REPRESENTS US!

Oballary '08

McCAIN IS A CYLON!

Panel 5: REPUBLICAN STRATEGISTS ARE STYMIED.

IT'D BE THE FIRST FEMALE AND BLACK PRESIDENT!

BUT IT'S ALSO WHITE AND MALE!

WITH DECADES OF COMBINED EXPERIENCE!

WHAT'LL WE DO?

Panel 6: NOT TO BE OUTDONE, McCAIN EXHUMES RONALD REAGAN'S HEAD TO WIN OVER WARY WINGNUTS!

DON'T WORRY... HE'S PLENTY CONSERVATIVE!

YOU TELL 'EM, RONNIE!

Just as I was putting the finishing touches on this strip, I found out that Tom Tomorrow had done the exact same premise with the Republican candidates the week before. We cartoonists have a term for the instances when multiple cartoonists inadvertently draw the same thing: a Yahtzee. My altie colleagues and I like to poke fun at the daily editorial cartoons for their frequent Yahtzees, which tend to involve the most obvious, hackneyed gags, but it sometimes happens to us too.

A few days later, I received a robocall from John McCain informing me that he is a proud conservative in the mold of Ronald Reagan. I had myself a good chortle.

See, this is one reason I'm a cartoonist instead of having a real job. All that increased worker productivity has helped lift corporate profits to record levels, yet in terms of real income, workers aren't sharing in the wealth they've created. Meanwhile, the incomes of even mediocre executives are ballooning like the force-fed geese used to make their *foie gras*. Screw that!

To give some idea of the concerns of the average Slowpoke reader, one wrote in to the *Village Voice* to defend the abacus, claiming his bookkeeper mother swore by its efficiency. How hard it is for us cartoonists not to offend!